OPERATION WARHAWKS

How Young People Become Warriors

by

Terrence Webster-Doyle

Atrium Society Publications
Middlebury, Vermont, USA

Atrium Society Publications
P.O. Box 816
Middlebury, VT 05753, USA

Cover Design:	Robert Howard
Editor:	Adryan Russ
Production Consultant:	Tom Funk
Creative Consultant:	Jean Webster-Doyle

Library of Congress Cataloging-in-Publication Data

Webster-Doyle, Terrence, 1940-
    Operation Warhawks : how young people become warriors / by Terrence Webster-Doyle; [illustrations, Rod Cameron].   p.   cm.
    Summary: Examines how people are conditioned to accept war as a way to settle disputes, discusses the effects of war and presents various nonviolent alternatives. Includes discussion questions and activities.
    ISBN 0-942941-30-6 (paper); ISBN 0-942941-31-4 (hardcover)
    1. Peace—Juvenile literature. 2. War—Juvenile literature. 3. Military socialization—Juvenile literature. 4. Militarism—Juvenile literature.
5. Pacific settlement of international disputes—Juvenile literature. [1. War. 2. Peace. 3. Militarism. 4. Conditioned response. 5. Conflict management.]
    I. Cameron, Rod, 1948-   ill.   II. Title.   JX1965.5.W43   1992
327.1'72-dc20   Library of Congress Catalog Card Number: 92-073959

Atrium publications are available at discount for bulk purchases or educational use. Contact Special Sales Director, Atrium Society, (800) 848-6021.

Printed in Singapore by Mandarin Offset

Dedication

To the innocent and trusting young people of the world,
who hope that we adults will begin to solve our problems
peacefully.

To a Dead Soldier

This is what happens
When you let a numskull run your country.
You should have known better
Than to vote for him.

But hey, I guess you always were a numskull, too.
Now look where it got you.
You died in a sandpit
Somewhere in the desert.
Now you just hang in limbo
And watch as life goes on all around you.

But it truly wasn't your fault, you know.
You had no choice in the matter.
You were conditioned from the day you were born
To do their bidding,
Conditioned to hate and fear the "enemy"
Whom you have never seen or spoken to,
But have been taught to hate all your life.

That is what went wrong.
There was nothing you could have done.
You were tricked into believing you were right.
Your thoughts were programmed from the start.

From day one you were taught what to do,
What to say, how to think and feel.
They taught you who to hate and who to serve. And you played right along.
You even believed.

And now you have broken away from their chains,
Now you can see the light...
All too clearly and much too late.

—*Stirling Dew , 17 years old*

TABLE OF CONTENTS

WHO CREATES WARRIORS?

WHAT ARE THE EFFECTS OF BEING A WARRIOR?

HOW CAN I AVOID BECOMING A WARRIOR?

With a Little Help from Our Friends

This book is written for you young people, ages 12 through 15, because this is an age when you may start thinking about war and the military more seriously. It is especially for those of you who might be considering joining the Armed Forces. This book is also written to help those of you who are younger. I have included some special sections for you, on war toys in particular. I share this book with you and the adults in your life. You, in turn, can share parts of the book with your younger brothers, sisters and friends, perhaps discussing what they mean. In this way each of us helps the next generation to stop using war as a way to solve the problems of human relationship.

Note to the Adult Reader

What is written in this book is a realistic and direct view of what creates warriors and war. To some, it may be very disturbing. There are adults who believe young people should not be burdened with this knowledge because it will frighten them. They feel young people should be protected from seeing what the world is really like. But young people today see tremendously frightening and violent movies, videos, magazines and television programs. They experience life on the streets, sometimes watching their friends get beaten up, scarred for life, or killed.

Showing young people the truth about violence, rather than glorifying it, helps them understand it. No matter what we do to try to prevent it, young people are going to see violence . Therefore, let's help them see what creates it and how they can avoid it. Let's help them think in healthier, more intelligent ways, which will help them act in those ways. We *can* help our children understand how we all create conflict and prevent peace from happening. The only question is—will we do it?

"Upon peace the very life of the world depends, perhaps even the progress or decay of our entire civilization."
—Maria Montessori, Educator

"Give me the first seven years of a child's life. . . "
—Adolph Hitler, Dictator

Foreword

THE DREAM OF GLORY

> *WARNING:*
> *BECOMING A WARRIOR MAY BE*
> *FATAL TO YOUR HEALTH*

This book is intended to disturb you, to "wake you up" so you can think seriously about the urge to become a warrior. War has been glorified by the media to make you think that being a warrior, a "hero" or "freedom fighter," is heroic, honorable and right. This is a terribly distorted view of what it is to be a warrior! These glorified views presented in movies, on television, in magazines and in video games are hypnotizing you, putting you to sleep, brainwashing you—in other words, "conditioning" you to think that the honorable solution to the problems of human relationship is through brutal, violent means. Being a warrior means killing men, women and children and destroying homes and cities, because we humans cannot find other, less violent ways to resolve our problems.

What is said and pictured in this book will perhaps shock you; at the least, it will make you question how human beings create warriors and war. Most adults, it seems, have "gone to sleep," have become brainwashed to accept that war is inevitable—that it cannot be avoided. This book questions conditioned (automatically accepted) beliefs about warriors and war.

As I wrote this book and designed the illustrations with

artist Rod Cameron, I worried about what effect it would have on you—the young reader. Some people believe that you should not be bothered with such issues as war, that you would not understand it. I disagree. I do not want to frighten you, but I do want you to see what you could be heading for. It is too late to present these issues to many older people. They already have their minds made up. But I hope you are young enough to question what you are being asked to believe and obey.

I cannot find words strong enough to describe how I feel about the horrors of war. Please understand that being a warrior is a deadly serious occupation. I am sure that if we think carefully and are truly concerned about each other we can resolve our problems in more intelligent and peaceful ways than by creating warriors and wars. I would like to develop a new occupation—*Peace Educator*—a person who studies the Art of Peace and teaches people how to avoid conflict and live happy lives. We have academies dedicated to the Art of War; we need to start academies dedicated to the Art of Peace.

As you read this book, please seriously consider what is being asked of you. Most importantly, QUESTION! For questioning will help free you from being put to sleep. If you are asleep, people can control you, even train you to be a killer! For thousands of years, people have been "put to sleep" and trained to go to war. Some people have kept themselves awake and tried to wake up others. You do not have to be brainwashed, to fall asleep—you too can keep awake by questioning. If you do fall asleep, waking up can be harsh, disturbing. The first step in "waking up" is to see that you are in a dream, that you have been put to sleep by being conditioned to accept unquestioningly the dreams of others, of society—dreams passed down from generation to generation. The dream is *only* that—a dream, just like you have at night as you sleep, except that it is daytime. Daydreaming may take many forms: the dreams of success, ambition, fame and fortune; the dreams of honor and duty, of defending one's homeland; dreams of heroes and enemies, good guys and bad guys; dreams of glory and patriotic action, and the social respect it brings.

The dream of glory, of being a warrior, is one that concerns me here. I, too, had been conditioned to dream this dream. I went to sleep and ended up being trained as a warrior. I woke up in the middle of it, and it was very harsh, very frightening. The dream was all I knew. For a long time after I woke up, I didn't know who I was or what I was supposed to be.

Now, being awake is wonderful! And yet I still see the sorrow, confusion and violence in those who are asleep, who live in their dream worlds of warriors and wars—a living nightmare played out each day with everyone convinced that it is all real and necessary. The terrible thing is that *none* of it is real or necessary. *It is only a dream!* And yet we carry out the horror of it year after year, generation after generation. This is why I have written this book, to wake you up, to show you that the dream of glory is a terrible illusion that we take to be real. Waking up can be disorienting, but if you are awakened because another cares about you, then I feel it will be all right.

And I do care about you—I do not want any young people to be hurt. You have probably already seen a tremendous amount of violence in the media. I am sorry that you have had to see it. It seems that many filmmakers only want to make lots of money by frightening you. I personally feel that they should be ashamed of what they do to hurt your minds.

Please see that this book is not trying to hurt you, but to help. I want to "creatively disturb" you so you will not become a warrior—so you will not kill or be killed. Being a warrior is a bad dream which could become a terrible nightmare if you go to war. If I can begin to wake you up with what is written and pictured here so you will question all those people who tell you that the way to peace is through war, then I have done my job. If only a few young people decide not to become warriors and hurt other human beings, I will feel happy.

It's now up to you. This book lies before you. It is an "adventure," a challenge to look at how young people like you become warriors. My only hope is that at the end you come away with the one most important question burning in your brain—

"Is there another way?"

A Real Dream

I'd like to tell you about a horrible experience that changed my life forever. At the time my life seemed changed for the worse, but now when I look back I see that my life changed for the better. Today, because of this experience, I am a saner, more intelligent, freer human being. When this experience occurred I was a young man and very "conditioned!"; that is, I believed unquestioningly in my role as a potential warrior, a "real man" who would defend a piece of land against all "enemies"—a warrior who would kill or die for his country.

When I grew up I was told by adults around me that "being a man," a cool, tough, aggressive person—a warrior—was good, noble, and even honorable. I saw that other young men were rewarded for their "honorable aggression," their power to command, take charge, be in control. But I couldn't quite be this man, this warrior type. I tried but it just didn't work. And yet for one very powerful, seemingly endless time, I gave in to the pressure of society to be a warrior—and I failed. At the time it hurt me terribly. I felt that I had let society down.

But that was then. Now I am dedicated personally and professionally to understanding why and how people like me are still being conditioned to become warriors. I want to question this conditioning so you, our new generation, don't have to go to war—to kill or be hurt or killed. I tell you this story not out of bitterness but out of care for you, so that you won't have to suffer the fears and horrors of being a "Warhawk."

DARK OF ENDLESS NIGHT

The alarm bells sounded! Men were running to their battle stations. The plane above was diving in for the attack! I didn't know where to go. I was panicked. Everyone else seemed to know what to do. The five-inch guns moved into position. With a deafening thunder of black-orange smoke, they belched their payloads of death.

The other ships were moving into position, their blue-black metal hulls like great fortresses at sea plowing through the deep Atlantic ocean waves. The plane was screaming down at us as the convoy of ships thundered back with rounds and rounds of cannon fire intermixed with more rapid bursts from smaller guns bristling over the ship's surface from where they were mounted.

As my ship, a destroyer, exploded with ammunition from its huge guns, it sent us rocking sideways. The seas were rough, causing the ship to plow under the wave top in a pitch and roll. But there was no time to feel these effects. Only shock, panic and an intense sensation of being in a nightmare, as if I were an actor in a war movie, looking disbelievingly at this bizarre scene—a strange, unreal feeling mixed with paralyzing fear.

What was I to do? It was my first day aboard the ship. I was just out of Basic Training. Before then, what had been expected of me was either to go to college, get a job or join the Armed Forces. I didn't think I could get into college with my poor grades, and I didn't want to get some hard, low-paying, boring job. That left the Armed Forces. I chose the Navy because I wanted to sail the seas and visit foreign lands. This was my only choice—or so I thought.

The shrill sound of sirens and the blaring of alarm horns mixed with sea and gunpowder odors all rocked violently in a huge metal ship armed to do two jobs—defend itself and its inhabitants and kill other humans with exploding bombs and flesh-splitting, bone-crushing bullets. I was awake, but it felt like a bad dream.   In a way, it was.

As I saw it, all the people on this ship of war
were asleep,
acting out their unconscious, conditioned roles,
being good little soldiers and sailors,
performing like people had trained them
and expected them to act,
killing other human beings they labeled "the Enemy."

Not one of them stopped to ask: What are we fighting over? Is there another way? Aren't we both doing the same thing—protecting and defending our country? What is the sense in all this? Who is the real enemy?

I knelt down beside one of the turrets of the many smaller gun posts on the ship. Clips of shells were being passed up to the gunner and injected into the rapidly firing, two-muzzle gun twisting around to follow the path of the incoming "enemy" plane. Ships were frantically circling, puffing out great billows of black smoke. Powerful explosions were turning the blue sky a patchwork of black and grey clouds. The plane kept on coming! Thoughts raced through my mind: "What should I do? No one told me where I was supposed to go." More panic. I didn't

18

want anyone to see me—to see that I didn't know what to do, that I had no role in this madness!

How did I get here? All had gone well back in Basic Training. I was chosen to be Master-At-Arms, an honored position. It was my job to make sure that these eighty men in my company were in order. I had to check the barracks for cleanliness. Everything was to be spotless—not a speck of dust or dirt to be found. Every day at regular times, and sometimes by surprise at night in the middle of a deep sleep, we were called to attention for an inspection: the company commander would go through our barracks to check on order. I was personally responsible to him to make sure everything was done perfectly.

After Basic Training, I wanted to serve on submarines but found out that I couldn't due to a bad injury to my liver from a car accident while in high school. So I was transferred to a destroyer—a fighting ship. But the strangest thing happened at that time. Although it really scared me then and caused me much mental strain, it has helped me become free of pain and suffering. As I get older I see more clearly how this one small experience opened my eyes in the middle of a bad dream and saved me from living a life that was destructive.

After a two-week leave which I spent at home following Basic Training, I was on my way to my new assignment—to serve on a Navy destroyer. I was deeply worried about this, but didn't show it outwardly. Deep inside me there was a troubled rumbling—a fearful discontent beginning to awaken. For years, my feelings of discontent had created much misery for me. They caused me to be a rebel, to shun all the ways society was trying to get me to be a "good" young man, a person who would serve his country, get a responsible job, practice

19

religion regularly, get married and be a model member of the community in which I lived. My discontent drove me to reject all this, to rebel by drinking and being wild, much to the disapproval of my parents, teachers and community leaders. Something was pushing me from deep inside. It was causing me great pain, but I just couldn't seem to help it.

There came a time when I had to make a choice: Do I continue rebelling and end up being the "no-good bum" they used to call me? Or do I now try to be "good"? At that moment I felt panic. The path was clear. I *had* to be good. I *had* to be a respected member of society and to conform to its demands. The deep rumbling was squashed with a fear I shall never forget. The pressure was immense. It was do or die! I wasn't going to be an outcast. That was too much to bear! Everyone around me was telling me, "Don't mess up your life!" "Conform!" "Be good!" So I became good—*really* good. I was going to be the best—an honored citizen, a hero. Joining the Navy was going to be the way I was going to prove this to everyone. But I was young and didn't understand all this at the time. It seemed something greater than myself was moving inside me.

It was a hot, humid summer day when I got aboard the bus to my new assignment. I felt extreme excitement mixed with a profound dread—and underneath it all, a deep depression. I didn't realize it then, but I was about to go through a profound and long-lasting change.

I stopped in a small town to catch a different bus. The bus station was dark and dirty with a few people waiting, sitting, lonely in separate parts of the large room. My bus was departing in two hours—in early evening. As I sat down, a sudden tiredness came over me, an exhaustion that was so deep

20

and so over-whelming that there was no fighting it. It was as if I hadn't slept in years. It felt like I imagine death to be. I fell into the deepest sleep that I have ever felt in my life, then or since. I recall no dreams, just complete emptiness. I awoke hours later to a vacant bus station. A few dirty, yellow lights glowed as I looked at the large, old clock on the wall. It was one o'clock in the morning! My bus had left hours ago! I was A.W.O.L! —"absent without leave." Panic hit me! What will happen to me? Will I be court-martialed? Sent to the brig, the Navy jail? Even worse, will I be shot for desertion? My mind was not rational. It was not thinking clearly. These intense, crazy thoughts raced through my brain. I will be a failure! A coward! Society will reject me! I will never make it! I'll die!

I tried to get up but I couldn't move! My legs were like cement. Nothing seemed to work. My eyelids felt as if they had two huge weights attached to them, and it was impossible to keep them open. I struggled in vain to get up.

**Sleep overcame me, pulled me down
into the dark of endless night, and held me there
until it was certain of the death of the person I once was.**

The next morning I awoke to the light of day coming in from the dingy windows of the bus station. No one had tried to make me move. I had slept there for sixteen hours! People moved about, buses were waiting in stalls for their passengers, and I lay there blinking, unknowingly, staring up at the ceiling. My body felt as light as a feather, as if a great, great weight had been lifted off me. And I felt a tremendous sense of relief and well-being as if the whole world were finally good and right. Not since I was very young had I felt this way before—feeling the wonder and joy of living in the excitement of each moment. Now I didn't care what happened to me. I felt alone, but not lonely. I felt completely free and wonderful—as if I had awakened at last from a long, bad dream, and everything was all right.

But it wasn't. Although miraculously nobody had noticed that I had been gone for so many hours, I was now back on assignment in the middle of the greatest nightmare of all. Great metal ships were exploding with cannon fire, trying to destroy that one, lonely plane that kept diving at us again and again. Those ships were firing tons of ammunition at it. I was in the middle of a nightmare, but I was wide awake in this one. And in my new state of awakeness, I could see that these people, running back and forth, were asleep, acting out the roles they had been trained for since birth. I could see their brainwashing. I could see that they were conditioned to believe that exploding cannon fire was right, honorable and good. I could see that they believed that they had to destroy and kill the enemy and defend their country, their race, their beliefs.

I could see that the "enemy" was just like us.
He believed that what he was doing
was noble, courageous,
right and good—
that he was defending his country, his race, his beliefs,
and that *he* was the freedom fighter and *we* were the
terrorists.

In his mind, *he* was the hero, and *we* were the enemy. I could see clearly that we were all living one-sided nightmares that did not take into consideration the humanity of the other human beings with whom we share this planet.

It was almost too overwhelming to see like this. Until now, I had been pretending to be like them, because I was afraid that they would see I was not "asleep" like them and terrified that they would see me as their "enemy" and punish me.

I *was* seen, and I *was* punished—but in a very different way. All this "war" we had just been exposed to was only pretend—a practice session for the Navy. Although the huge shells were real, the plane was not. It was controlled by electronics with no pilot. At the end of this exercise it crashed into the sea without being hit.

The next morning I went to the medical corpsman, the person in charge of the medical facility on the ship, and told him I could no longer stay on the ship. When he asked me why, I said that I felt sick inside and couldn't serve in the Navy any longer. Mental tests were given to me. The Navy psychiatrist saw me twice and said, on the second meeting, that I needed to leave the Navy. I was then sent to a veteran's hospital, to Ward E32 where some men took away all my belongings and gave me a bathrobe, slippers and pajamas. They locked me up behind two sets of double-locked doors with windows protected by screens that would never open. I was kept there for two months, and they were unquestionably two of the longest months of my life.

I saw things that I shouldn't have, like the man who woke up in the middle of the night screaming, "They are coming to get me, Captain!" He had fought in the Korean War and was having nightmares because of his experiences. The Navy "treated" him by tying his hands and feet with leather straps, spread-eagle, to the four corners of the bed. There he lay all night thrashing and screaming, wide-eyed and crazed while the leather straps dug deeply into his wrists and ankles. Another night, in the bed across from me, a young man had a fit. He arched his back and bounced on his bed until the medical assistants came and held him down. They jammed a taped wooden stick in his mouth, part way down his throat—apparently so he wouldn't bite his tongue in half. There was a boy who tried to kill himself by cutting his wrists and another boy who could barely move, his body covered with open wounds caused by extreme stress and fear. Another time a medical assistant took one of the boys and put him into a "padded" cell. The boy was wrapped in a straightjacket, a white canvas coat that has extra long arms with leather straps at the ends that are tied behind. The jacket was put on him from the back and securely laced up. His arms were wrapped in the jacket and secured across his chest in a self-hugging position, then tied very tightly behind him. The medical assistant said they did this so he could not harm himself.

To me, it didn't look like a form of protection. To me, it looked like punishment for these "crazy" young men who couldn't function in the military any longer. I saw that they were sensitive, intelligent young men who had difficulty being what society called "a man"—the violent, brutal image men are expected to be. Like me, it was not in them to be aggressive, competitive cut-throats. I saw in the eyes of the Navy that we were the rejects, the cowards, the deserters, the outcasts. I was so ashamed, and I was afraid that my family and friends would find out.

After two months of being locked up—seeing young men go crazy, trying to kill themselves, and get punished for being sick—they finally let me go. I left the Navy base and took nothing more than the clothes I wore. Everything else I left on the floor by my locker. I was given some money to take the train home.

I walked up the steps to my parents' apartment, let myself in, went directly to my room and locked my bedroom door. I was home in no time, but getting over that experience took me years.

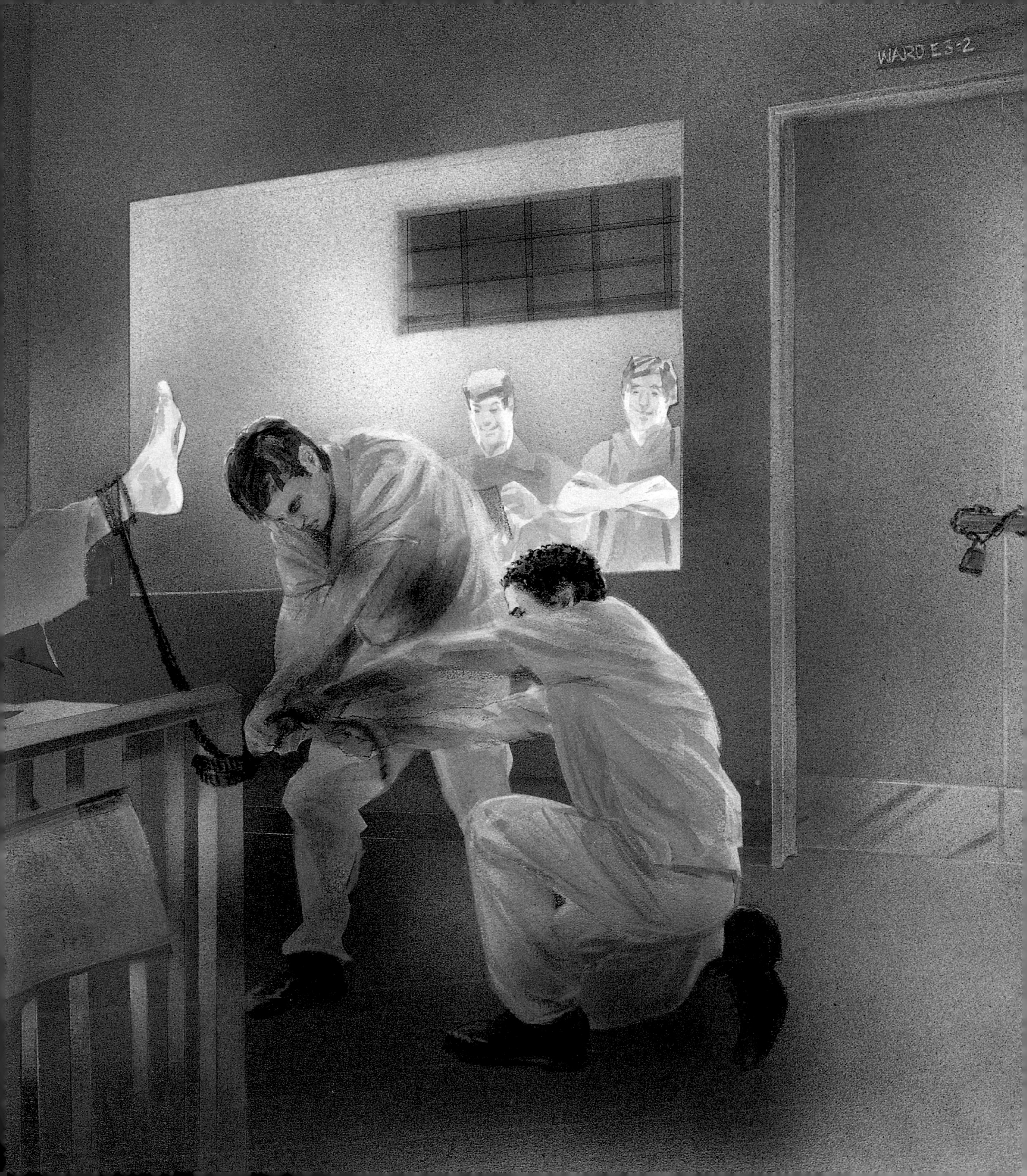
WARD E3-2

WHO CREATES WARRIORS?

Chapter 1

WAR—THE FINAL ENEMY

Greetings to you, young readers worldwide!

The story you have just read is true. While it is now many years later, I continue to feel the powerful effect of the experience to this day. When I read the story now, if I want to remember I can feel the pain and depression it caused me then. Even if I could speak many languages, I'm not sure I could find a way to tell all of you the feelings that stirred inside me while training to become a military person—a warrior.

The men who suffered in that military hospital and during wartime were healthy young people before they became conditioned to fight, kill and even die. They became sick because of a sickness in society, a sickness that says young people must join the military and become warlike. Many people just can't take that kind of pressure. They become ill trying to live up to the image society has of them—to be a warhawk.

I am writing this book to give you information that could prevent you from being hurt—emotionally and physically. I have friends who have had the experience of being in real wars. Some lived through them and some died. The ones who lived will never forget; all are scarred for life. They remember the horror of killing other people. Some remember the insane moments of having to stop another human being with a bayonet. The descriptions I've heard about killing have made me feel great sorrow and disbelief. The many war stories these people know would make you cry, and cry again.

What I went through was not as bad as real war and real killing. Basic Training was enough for me. Every time I contemplate what I went through, along with stories of those who fought in wars, nagging questions go around and around in my brain. Why do we kill each other? How do we become warriors? What makes us want to shoot, stab, bomb other human beings? I cannot imagine what this would be like. It doesn't seem real to me. It's like a dream, a nightmare that we will someday wake up from. I keep on wondering: *Aren't there other ways for human beings to relate to each other without fighting?*

In this book, we will look at these questions and look at how we have been trained throughout our early years to become warriors. All of us—boys, girls, women and men—have been trained to believe something that is the cause of all wars: that there are enemies that must be killed to preserve our particular way of life.

I absolutely reject war as a solution to human problems.
I cannot understand how anyone can accept war
for *any* reason.
It is an insane, barbarous act!
I know there are humane, sane ways to solve conflict.
You, however, must understand this for yourself.

In order to understand this, we will look at:

○   How we have been conditioned to accept conflict as a fact of life.

○   The influences that encourage us to use violence as a way to resolve conflict.

○   How we have been trained to believe violence and war are honorable ways to resolve human problems.

○   What you can do to end war—in yourself and in the world.

I love this beautiful earth and its wonderful living things. I want only to preserve it and help you young people to live healthy, happy lives in its surroundings. I live in the United States—a part of the world that has great beauty, which, of course, I want to see endure. I have traveled to other parts of the world and I have seen beauty in all those countries as well. But throughout the world, I have also seen horror, suffering and tremendous ignorance and grief.

This horror, ignorance and grief *can* end. The way it can end is for us to understand that:

❶   *We* create this horror, ignorance and grief; therefore *we* can understand it..

❷   The way to stop creating this suffering is to learn to see *how* we create it.

❸   If we can question these things together, there is a possibility of solving our problems peacefully.

Understanding begins with *you* and *me*—each one of us individually and all of us together. Understanding how we are conditioned to become warriors will help us understand how we create conflict and war.

In this book, we will ask many questions. It is only through questioning that we can begin to understand.

Must we have war?
Just because we have always had war
since the beginning of human time,
must we continue to have it?

I do not condemn any person (military or non-military) who believes we must have war. At one time I was conditioned to believe it, and I know I wasn't bad for believing it. I no longer believe it, however, and want to show you why. We have been taught to believe that war is inevitable. In so doing, we have created tremendous conflict in the world. To begin to resolve our conflict, we need to understand how we were taught (conditioned) to believe this way. The only way to understand what we believe is to *ask questions.*

Do you know the meaning of "belief"? I looked it up in a dictionary. It means "conviction of the truth or reality of a thing, based upon grounds insufficient to afford positive knowledge." This means you believe something even though you have no proof that it's true. You act blindly, without finding out for yourself, without questioning, without knowing first-hand. When someone says something is true, you believe it and follow that person, making that belief your "ideal," your security, your truth. You may even defend it, never knowing whether it is actually true.

It is very important that you question, that you find out for yourself what is true. As you read this book *and throughout your life*, ask questions. By questioning rather than immediately accepting or believing what another tells you, you uncover the truth of a situation for yourself.

Believing without questioning is dangerous! It is one of the ways wars happen!

Activity: Asking Questions

✓ Think of a subject you have questions about. For example: war, peace, nature, atomic bombs, the military, movies, television, games.

✓ Ask yourself what you'd like to know about your subject.

✓ Write down every question you can think of regarding your subject. For example, if your subject is "war":
1. How does war get started?
2. How is the enemy created?
3. Why do people decide to become warriors?
4. What is war good for?
5. Which countries have benefited from war? Why?
6. Do I have to go to war?
7. Should war be outlawed?

✓ Get answers to your questions. Ask family members or ask your teacher to set up a library visit or a visit from a guest lecturer, so that you can get answers to the questions you have written down.

✓ Talk about the answers you find and how you got them. Discovering new information is exciting and fun!

✍ ✍ ✍

REMEMBER:
The most important thing you can do is:
Q U E S T I O N!

Questions about "Dark of Endless Night":

1. Do you think training for the armed services is a violent experience?

2. How does it make you feel to think of someone as "the enemy" and be trained to kill that enemy?

3. Have you sometimes felt torn between being "good" and rebelling? What kind of thoughts have run through your mind about it?

4. Did you know that the Armed Forces lock up people who don't conform to their wishes, as if they were prisoners?

5.   What did you think of the "ill" men who had night-mares from their war experiences?

6.   What must their war experiences be like to cause such terrible nightmares and reactions?

7.   How do you think men and women feel when they must return home unable to face military life?

8.   Do you think they ought to feel guilty or ashamed?

9.   If someone you know returned home after Basic Training unable to take any more military experiences, how would you react to the person? Reject him or her as a coward? Honor him or her as a real patriot?

10. If someone decides that war is insane and training to be a warrior is destructive to all that is loving and intelligent, what should they do or say about it?

11. Why do people give other people awards and medals for killing?

12. Why do people celebrate war, "victories" of murder?

Chapter 2

THE ANCIENT WARRIORS

Who creates war? Our enemies? Our generals? Our politicians? As I have said, the truth is that war is created by you and me. I know this may surprise you, but this is how it happens. Every time we think, and every time we act on what we think, we have the potential to either create war or create peace. In order to understand how we got this way, let's look at a simple version of how it all began.

Let's go back in time to when humans were simple cave creatures who had to hunt food to survive. It is here that our need for warriors and war began. Please note: What is written about war in this book is a general outline. If you have an interest in studying in-depth causes of war, I have written two other books for young people: *Tug of War: Peace through Understanding Conflict* and *Fighting the Invisible Enemy: Understanding the Effects of Conditioning.*

In the Beginning

Hundreds of thousands of years ago, human creatures lived a very primitive life. There was constant danger. Humans were sometimes eaten by wild animals and attacked by other humans. In order to survive, which is what we are driven to do, those early human creatures decided that to protect themselves from wild beasts and other human creatures, they would join together in small groups called tribes. They felt there was safety in numbers.

In order to make sure that the tribe stayed together, they developed a system of relating to each other that was unique to their group. They developed different symbols of recognition—such as wearing blue feathers in their hair or bear teeth around their necks for "identification." Like today's gang colors or national flags, such an identification let others know that they belonged to a specific tribe.

As tribes grew larger and the need to extend tribal hunting grounds grew, the tribes were faced with a new problem. Survival meant eating, and since there was just so much food to go around, especially in times of drought and other natural disasters that limited the food supply, tribes fought over limited resources. The tribe that won was the biggest, strongest, best-equipped, and best-organized.

In order to remain the biggest, strongest, best-equipped and organized, a tribe had to develop certain rituals and beliefs that kept the group together. If anyone left the tribe, the group would grow weaker. Tribal leaders worked hard to keep the tribe together. Each member was conditioned to think and act together and be like the others. In certain ways, such as planting crops, hunting or building, working together as a tribe was beneficial. In other ways, it caused problems and sometimes led to conflicts that escalated into great battles. These wars happened because, forced to think and act alike within a particular tribe or group, people could not be friends with people of other tribes.

Example: Blue Feathers vs. Green Feathers

When someone from a tribe that wore blue feathers would not let a stranger wearing green feathers eat some of the food he found even though both were hungry, they got into a fight.

A Definition of Enemy: A Person Who Is Different

Over the years the tribes grew, the battles went on, and the concept of "enemy" came into being. The enemy was that person or those persons who were different, unlike you and your tribe. They were, therefore, considered a threat to you as well as your tribe. What affected you, affected the tribe. What affected the tribe, affected you.

Battles were fought, wars were declared, and conditioning grew stronger and deeper. Tribe members in future generations continued to fight one another, even though they had long forgotten what they were fighting about. They just continued to act in conditioned ways without asking questions.

As these tribes grew larger over the centuries, they became nations and countries and developed even more complicated systems of beliefs to hold them together. From time to time, many individuals tried to untangle these systems of belief but wound up creating new ones instead, creating more confusion and conflict. Now, hundreds of thousands of years later, we humans are still conditioned to survive by identifying with a particular group or tribe, and we are still fighting.

Questions:

1. Can you think of some groups or tribes with which you associate yourself today?

2. Is your school like a tribe? Your community or home? Is your nation like a tribe?

3. What is something you believe in that you share with other members of a group?

4. Does this shared belief separate you somehow from other people who do not share this belief?

5. Have you ever thought of someone as an "enemy"? What circumstances made you think of that person as an "enemy"?

6. Have you ever felt conflict because of a difference in beliefs?

7. What can we do about this kind of conflict?

8. Do you think it helps when members of different groups or tribes talk to one another to work out their differences?

9. What would they need to do to listen to each other?

10. What would they say to each other?

The Ways We Create Conflict

Let's look some more at this need to identify with a group. Let's break it down into small parts to see, step-by-step, how identification with a group (tribe, clan, nation, race, etc.) creates conflict. Is there a basic pattern that we humans have adhered to since the beginning of our existence, a pattern shared by all human beings, which separates the human race? If we can understand this pattern, we can see how conflict begins. It begins with our strong desire to survive:

Our First Pattern of Conflict

❶   **I want to survive!**

❷   **In order to survive, I must join a group (tribe).**

❸   **If I identify with that group, I will be protected, safe from harm.**

❹   **When I identify with the group:**

- ○ **I isolate myself from others outside my group.**
- ○ **I judge outsiders' behavior, which is not like mine, to be "bad."**
- ○ **In judging someone else as bad, I cause separation between that person and myself.**

❺ **In causing separation, I create an "enemy."**

❻ **By creating an enemy, I create conflict and war.**

Let's look at this pattern in greater detail. Conflict and war are created through:

❶ **Identification**
I condition myself to think and act in a particular way—a "good," acceptable way, along with a cluster of other people. This group becomes "US."

❷ **Projection**
Like a movie projector, I *project* "bad" behavior onto anyone not with me or like me or the group I have joined. Those people not like us or with us become "the enemy"—"THEM."

Here is an example of how identification works to create conflict:

Example: Let's say that you see your friends going to a particular kind of religious place (a "church") on a particular day (a "Sunday"). What might be your reaction to seeing this if you do not belong to any religious group?

This experience might make you feel:

- You are an outsider
- You are lonely or afraid
- You want to belong to that particular group so you can feel comfortable, secure, unafraid
- Or you could say I have my own group and I feel secure so it does not really matter what "they" do.

Perception (Sight): "There go my friends into that group's building."

Conception (Thought): "I am an outsider."

Emotion (Feeling): "I feel lonely, insecure, afraid."

Where does this come from? As you just learned, it comes from an old tribal need to join together for survival. This was and still is necessary, but today survival depends on the *whole* world cooperating as one "tribe," all human beings depending on each other. Our inherited memory tells us that survival means separate groups (nations, races, religions); our intelligence tells us that this is an old, outdated way of survival that doesn't work any longer.

Here is an example of how projection works to create conflict.

44

Example: The Black and White Dog

Let's say you see a black and white dog that looks mean. Suppose the dog bites you. This experience, which frightens you, registers on your brain, almost like a movie camera filming an event.

A week later, you see a different black and white dog. This time the dog is friendly, but what happens in your brain? Do you experience fear? The desire to protect yourself? Where does the fear come from? This dog? Or from your memory of the past?

Perception (sight):
"There is a black and white dog."

Conception (thought):
"That is a dangerous dog!"

Emotion (feeling):
"I'm afraid I'll be bitten again!"

The Pattern:
**Your perception (seeing the dog) + conception (remembering the dangerous dog)
+ emotion (fear of being hurt) = need to defend or attack**

Your memory tells you that this dog is dangerous when, in fact, this particular dog is not. Because of your first experience with a black and white dog, your mind (thought/memory) has developed a *prejudice* about black

and white dogs. Like a movie *projector* your brain projects the image of hostility onto the dog.

The Enemy

In this same way, we look at a person and judge that person to be an "enemy." Look at the pattern that is created in your mind when you are conditioned to believe that someone is an enemy. You feel fear, a desire to protect yourself, to defend yourself, and—finally—your brain decides there is only one way to protect and defend yourself: eliminate the enemy.

The Pattern:

Other Person = Enemy

|

Enemy = Fear

|

Fear = Protect = Defend = Eliminate

Can you see how we create conflict by the way we think and then act (identification and projection, for example)? This is actually a *mechanical process* in the human brain—the brain of *all* human beings. We have been conditioned to act like robots, to automatically react to programs that have been put into our brains. We feel fear, the program is activated, the enemy is created, the need for protection is stimulated and the war is on.

Here is an activity that can help you understand how the brain creates fear of the "enemy."

✍ ✍ ✍

Activity: Attack of The Terminator

✓ Think of an image that makes you feel afraid.

✓ Now think of where this fear comes from. A past experience? Something you read? A movie you saw? A memory?

✓ What's your first reaction to the feeling of fear? Do you want to forget it? Run away? Hide? Fight it? Smother it?

✓ Is there an "enemy" connected to this feeling of fear? Who is this enemy?

✓ What do you want to do to this enemy? If there is no enemy, what do you want to do to make this feeling go away?

✓ Your fear is the Terminator! You have been attacked by the Terminator! Your brain created this fear, just like it created the image, "enemy." "Fear" and "enemy" are *images*—in your mind!

✓ The Terminator (fear) terminates (ends, gets rid of) open-

48

mindedness, intelligence, awareness in relationship.

✓ If your brain automatically reacts with prejudice and fear, you lose your ability to use intelligence and to understand what is happening to you.

✓ By allowing the Terminator to create an "enemy" in your mind, you prevent peace!

**We *prevent* peace
by the way we think and act.**

Once we truly understand what prevents peace, war will be no more. The warrior will be out of a job!

The following is an activity to reveal what *prevents* peace. It is similar to the one you just did, but it is designed to help you with situations that bring about fear and show you another way to deal with it.

✍ ✍ ✍

Activity: Terminate the Terminator

✓ Select an image that creates fear in you. Perhaps a person, a situation that happened to you, or a nightmare.

✓ Think of that frightening image, sit quietly and calm your mind by counting your breaths. Focus your attention on your breathing and count from one to ten, then over again. Do this for a few minutes until the frightening images start to fade.

✓ Now, look at the image again. Look at the image as if you were watching a movie or program on television. Look at it as if it were nothing more than an image on a screen.

✓ Remind yourself that this image *cannot* hurt you. Realize that it has no control over you. It is *just* an image!

✓ See the scary image come up. If it's a person, talk to that person. Tell "it" that you are not afraid. Tell "it" a joke to make it laugh. Try to change the image in your mind. If it's big, make it small. If it looks mean or violent, make it gentle and loving.

✓ The more you practice this, the more confident you will be that these fears, these Terminators, will not control you.

✓ Now, terminate the Terminator! Say "Hi!" to your fear, and then tell it, "Goodbye!" Let it come in, watch it as if it were a movie, then let it go out. That's all.

✍ ✍ ✍

Questions:

1. What is projection, and how does it create conflict?

2. What happens when you are told over and over that a certain person, a certain country, race or religion is evil or dangerous or a threat to you, your family and friends?

3. What happens in your brain? Does this information become a permanent film or program in your brain? Does it become stored away as memory?

4. What label or category does the computer in your brain apply to this "other" person, race or religion?

5. Does fear create the enemy? How?

6. When the brain "calls up" that stored information from its memory banks and sees someone as an "enemy," do you feel warlike or peaceful?

7. Can you see that anyone you consider an "enemy" also has "enemies" and that in the eyes of this enemy, you too may be an enemy?

8. What is identification?

9. How was it used in the past to create security?

10. Does it work now, or does it prevent security?

11. What can you do to end identification?

12. In order to end war, do you think we have to see where it starts?

13. In seeing it, do you think we can end it right there, at the root?

14. If we understand the conflict inside us, do you think we can understand conflicts that happen outside us?

15. Can you understand what is being asked of you here? If not, who can help you understand this? (Is it important enough to you to ask someone? If you do ask someone, remember: don't let them tell you *what* to think; the idea is for you to *understand how you think* and how it might create conflict.)

Chapter 3

OPERATION WARHAWK—CREATING A WARRIOR

How Do We Create Warriors?

In this section, we are going to do a "science project" called "Operation Warhawk." In this experiment you will need to imagine that you will be taking an "empty robot" and creating a warrior (like Dr. Frankenstein did to create the "monster"). You will be given the "parts" or "pieces" (nuts and bolts) to put together this robot (which can be either a man or woman robot—for this operation or experiment it will be a "man"—for this has been the typical warrior in the past. Sadly, now women warrior robots are being made.)

Let's see what we come up with—remember your job is to build and program a warrior—to "condition" it with all the necessary things that will make it do what you want: to kill! Your robot starts out with nothing in its memory banks (like a baby). Whatever "data" you expose to your robot will be stored away in its memory banks, so that when confronted by a new situation it will be able to sort through its memory to decide how to behave. By the time your "adult" robot is ready to perform, its memory banks will be full of a great deal of material to help it "think" and act.

Remember a very important fact: without warriors, there can be no wars. Who is the warrior? What is a warrior made of? Let's create this warrior, from scratch! Then we'll know!

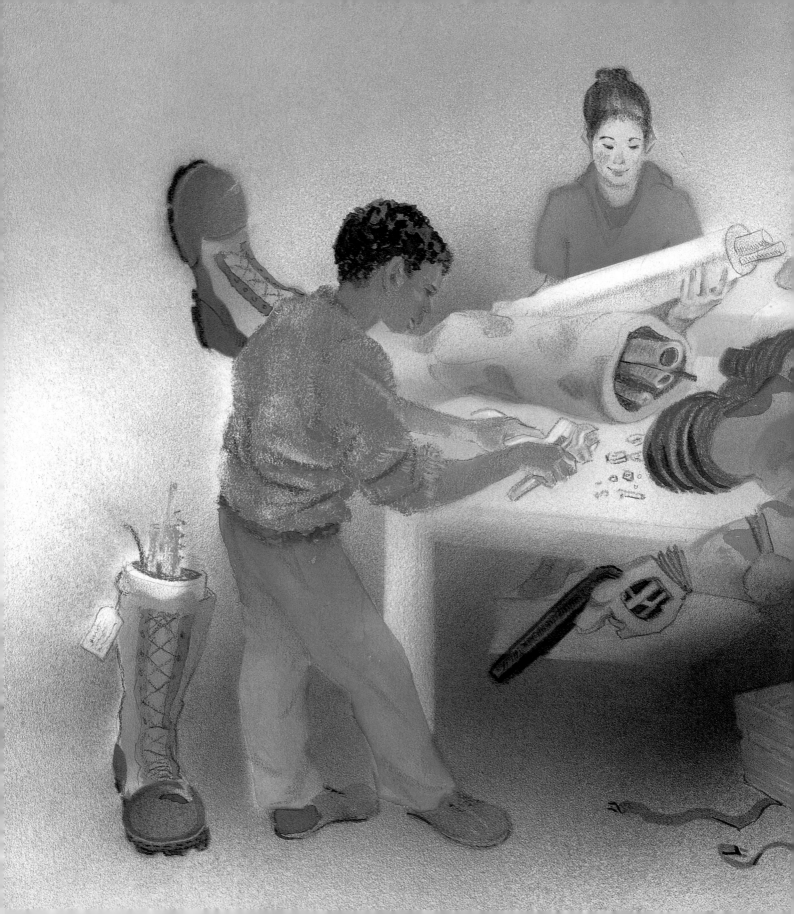

✑   ✑   ✑

Activity: Operation Warhawk—a Science Project

✓   Pretend you are a scientist, an inventor. Your project is to create a warrior, a robot that will kill other people when you say so. Let's call this robot Warhawk.

✓   How would you turn this robot into an armed, trained killer?

✓   What would you have to do to make Warhawk think like a military soldier?

✓   Supposing Warhawk has a computer for a brain, how would you train it, brainwash it, condition it?

✓   What kinds of thoughts would Warhawk think? What kinds of words would Warhawk say? How would Warhawk act?

✓   Read the rest of this chapter to help you with your experiment.

✑   ✑   ✑

The "Child" Robot Warrior

1. Warhawk starts out as a child robot. Where will you get programmed information to fill his brain and help him react "properly" on the battlefield some day when he is an adult robot?
    —War comics?
    —War movies?
    —War games and videos?
    —War toys?
    —War hero images?

2. Will you need to create the young Warhawk's allegiance to a flag (a symbol of tribal identification) and country (a tribal territory) as well as a desire to defend these to the death, if necessary?

3. Will the young Warhawk need to be programmed to feel honorable reasons to go to war?

4. Will child Warhawk need to learn how to get angry, violent, tough?

5. Will this robot have to learn how to fight, punch, kill?

6. Who will Warhawk's heroes be?

7. Will this warrior play with toys that encourage fighting?

8. What lessons do you hope to teach the robot when he watches those cartoons on television in which pretend creatures fight instead of working out solutions to their problems?

9. Will Warhawk have to learn to love violence? If so, how?

10. What normal, healthy human responses to fear and violence will need to be eliminated from your robot so it can automatically kill?

The Adult Robot Warrior

❶ To program Warhawk to grow into an adult warrior, will you need to teach the warrior to be:
    —Tough?
    —Cool?
    —Unfeeling?
    —In charge or in control?
    —The boss?
    —Fearless?

❷ Will Adult Warhawk believe that:
    —Might is right?
    —Death is preferable to dishonor?
    —Country and race come first?
    —It's important to be aggressive and competitive with other people?

❸   Will your adult robot:
>—Follow orders or give them?
>—Respect all authority or ask questions?
>—Hang around other warriors or mix with all kinds of people?
>—Handle problems with brawn or try to talk them out?

Warrior Language

Robot Warrior Slogans:

"Mess with the best, die with the rest."
"Death before dishonor!"
"My life for frcedom!"
"Kill 'em all, and let God sort 'em out!"
"Mercenaries never die, they just go to Hell to regroup."
"Peace through tyranny!"

Special Warrior Doubletalk:

- Friendly fire (killing your own troops by mistake)
- Smart bombs (bombs with computerized tracking capability)
- Military intelligence (thinking of ways to kill)
- Freedom fighters (terrorists)
- Cookie cutter (Neutron bomb)
- Peacemaker (MX missile)

- Christmas Tree Farm (24 nuclear-armed missiles on a Trident submarine)
- Star Wars or Peace Shield (a nuclear "umbrella" of bombs to blow up incoming "enemy" bombs)
- "Little Boy" and "Fat Man" (names of the two Atomic bombs that fell on Hiroshima and Nagasaki during the Second World War)
- Ethnic cleansing (killing people)

Can you think of others? Have you seen others in newspapers or heard them used on television news broadcasts? Are acts of extreme violence hidden in "friendly" terms?

Special Warrior Training

Then you will have to put Warhawk through special warrior training so it can learn how to kill:
- Put it into a room with other robots.
- Give it the same uniform as the others have.
- Take away anything that makes it look like an individual robot.
- Humiliate and harass your robot constantly.
- Call your robot a "Momma's boy."
- Tell your male robot that female robots are soft, weak and good for only one thing.
- Tell your female robot it can wear a uniform but it will not be able to do everything a man does.
- Tell your robot it's a "real jock."
- Give your robot chants, pledges and rituals that make it sound like a grunting, primitive animal.

60

- Constantly march your robot with other robots, drilling them into unison, to act as one unit.
- Make them act automatically to orders; train them to obey without thinking.
- Put them through tests of their "manliness" by putting them through war games.
- Tell them they will be heroes and will be honored by their country if they fight.
- Tell them they will be cowards if they don't fight for their country.
- Tell them, "Freedom has a price—blood!"
- Teach them to master hand-to-hand combat, to go beyond the usual limits of self-control in order to hurt someone else.
- Tell them that their enemies are not fully human, so it's all right to eliminate them without feeling.
- Tell them they will send their enemies home to their Mommies in a "glad bag."
- Get them to chant "Kill! Kill! Kill!" over and over until they really feel it!
- Get them to believe that killing is just a job, that after their first one, it won't be so bad.
- Motivate them to want to kill so badly that they won't feel satisfied until they do it.
- Tell them that people will need to die to make the world free.
- Tell them that their loyalty is to their group only.
- Get their families and community, which also consist of robots, to support them in being a trained soldier, a killer.

- After they go to war and kill, give them medals to honor their killing and congratulate them on a "job well done!"
- Tell them, after all this, they are now heroes and patriots.

If you followed the directions correctly, whether your robot, Warhawk, is a boy or girl, a woman or man, it is now ready to do what you trained it for; it has been conditioned to kill other people when given the order to do so. Your experiment is a success; you are to be congratulated!

Freedom Fighters—How Warriors Feel Heroic by Killing Enemies

Did you know that creating warriors creates heroes? Let's look at this. We have learned how ancient warriors came about and how we create warriors today. Now let's look at how creating warriors creates heroes—because in order to do the terribly destructive acts for which a warrior is "built," a warrior will need to think that what he or she is doing is right, good and even helpful to his or her country, race, religion. In order to kill, warriors have to see themselves as the "good guys," the "Freedom Fighter," the "Heroes." Seeing themselves in this way, they can feel right in acting like killers. They can even give each other medals, awards and other honors for killing the enemy.

How does this happen?

Almost every country in the world has armed forces. Men and women all over the world are trained to protect themselves and their country or race by learning how to kill other people. They become "warriors." When one country's warriors feel threatened by another country's actions and fear for their survival, they begin to think of the other country's people as "bad." They separate themselves from the "others," make the "others" wrong in their minds and call them "enemy."

An interesting point about human nature is that as soon as our brain creates the image "enemy," we human beings feel the need to create an opposing force—a "hero." After we decide there is a "terrorist," something inside us says we must create a "freedom fighter"—someone who will save us from this "enemy." Therefore the need for the warrior. Let's look at it again.

> ### The Brain Pattern:
>
> **There is an enemy.**
> **This enemy is going to harm me.**
> **What can I do to protect myself?**
> **I need a hero!**
> **The hero is the one who can protect me.**
> **Let's create the hero warrior—a Freedom Fighter—**
> **to fight the enemy.**

This is where our peace-making abilities break down. At this point, our "old" primitive brain takes over—the one that tells us we must either fight or run away.

Instead of trying to resolve the conflict with this country we call "enemy" by understanding our differences or seeing how human beings have been divided through organized beliefs, we create warriors, tribes, battalions. The outcome? War!

Let's look at it once more —

❶ The people of one country (or race or religion) feel threatened by another.

❷ They think of that country (or race or religion) as "bad" or "wrong" and make it an enemy in their minds.

❸ They feel they must defend and protect themselves against this enemy.

❹ They decide they will need warriors!

❺ They have no choice but to go to war!

Can you see where the breakdown in thinking happens in this pattern of conflict? The following is an activity to help you understand this process in our brain that makes us want to go to war and to help you see what we can do to break the pattern.

Activity: Breaking the Enemy Image Pattern

✓   Think of a situation—at home, at school, in your community—in which you created some kind of enemy. (It could be a person, an animal, a situation, a nightmare, a country, a particular group.)

✓   Write down who or what that enemy was. Keep in mind that there is no enemy unless *you* create one.

✓   Ask yourself how you responded to this enemy. Did you become the "hero warrior," the "Freedom Fighter," and respond in some way to this enemy's behavior?

✓   As a result of your hero warrior response, what happened? Did the "enemy" then counter-attack in some way?

✓   Were you happy with the outcome of this situation? If it happened again today, would you act differently?

✓   Now, go back in your mind to the point at which you created the "enemy" in your mind.

✓   Break the enemy image by seeing what it is—*only an image!* What can you do to resolve the conflict so that this person or situation *never* becomes an "enemy"?

Questions:

1.   Do you think your robot knows how to solve the problems of human relationship? If not, why?

2.   Do you think your robot will know how to do anything more than go to war and kill other human beings, since the robot only can act automatically? How did this come about?

3   Will this robot do whatever it's told without asking questions? Why?

4.   Do you think there are people like these "robots"? Who? Where?

5.   Can you see the difference between a physical threat and a mental threat? What is it?

6.   Are you aware that "enemy" exists *only* in your mind—that there is no enemy unless you think someone is an enemy?

7.   Might fear be our only real enemy? Why?

8.   Do you think *you* create war? Can you think of a way you and your family create war at home?

9.   When a small conflict turns into a big one at your home, what happens?

10. When a small conflict escalates into a big one in our country, what happens?

11. Do you think wars begin with the image of "enemy"? If yes, how?

12. What is the best way to break the enemy image pattern?

13. How have we come to think that it is heroic, honorable and even beneficial to kill other human beings?

14. What made us think this way?

15. Is this like thinking that smoking cigarettes is *good* for our health?

16. Why don't we see the crazy way we think?

17. Who would want us to continue to think in this way? Why?

18. How would it benefit them?

19. Can we be controlled by certain people because of the way we have been conditioned to think?

20. Who can free us from our conditioned thinking?

Chapter 4

THE WAR MACHINE

Your classmates are no longer with you. You are on your own now. You are walking down a dark alley at night. You know you shouldn't have taken this shortcut home. There are no lights to see where you are going. You feel danger. Hair stands up on the back of your neck as you hear a sudden noise behind you. You turn quickly, heart beating fast, palms sweating, your mouth dry as you strain to see who is there. You want to call out but you are frozen in fear. You raise your clenched fists in anticipation of the threat you feel coming at you.

Out of the dark looms a large male figure. He looks shaggy and dirty. You see a bottle in his right hand. Your legs feel like cement. You want to scream and run, but you just watch transfixed by this large shaggy assailant. You are captured like a deer in the headlights of an oncoming car.

Just ten feet from you, he mumbles something through a drunken stupor. He raises his bottle in a threatening gesture. Suddenly your legs react—you turn and flee down the alley, around the dark corners, with the drunken man calling after you. Finally you make it to the main street and the safety of lights and people. You see and wave down a police patrol car. You describe your run-in and the police car takes off quickly for the alley. You stand there in the bright light of a street lamp, shaking, sweating, out of breath, your legs like rubber. It's a good thing you are a fast runner, a sprinter on your school track team. You are relieved to be out of danger. You notice that your hands are still clenched tightly in fists.

This is a simple example of a person reacting to fear, an experience that you've probably had at one time or another. An isolated, potentially threatening event created your reactions. Your hands sweated, you felt frozen, unable to speak; your heart was beating fast and your mouth went dry. These are symptoms of a fight-or-flight response to danger, that is, a way for you to survive a potential threat by either fighting or by running away. This automatic response is built into the brain for protection in situations that are a threat to your *physical* survival.

In "Martial Arts for Peace" (Chapter 14), we will explore how to stop a potential *physical* threat by neither fighting nor running away but by creating nonviolent alternatives to get out of this situation peacefully. For now let's look at another simple example of a threatening situation—not a real, immediate threat to physical survival but rather a threat to *psychological* survival.

You and your classmates are visiting a foreign country, walking down a street in the late afternoon. In front of you, a group of people are arguing. They are shouting at each other. As you come closer you see that there are two different groups, each with noticeably different skin color and style of dress. There is much noise, and no one is able to say anything without many others shouting at the same time.

"You are the terrorists and we are the freedom fighters! You are disbelievers, infidels. God will punish you. We are chosen ones. Our place in history and our holy books make us God's favorites," one group shouts to the other.

"No! You have it all wrong. We are the freedom fighters and *you* are the terrorists. God is on *our* side, he has chosen *our* race as the inheritors of his will on earth. All those that disagree will be punished by the will of God."

You suddenly realize one of the groups is familiar to you. They all wear a symbol on a chain around their necks, the same symbol your parents and relatives at home have around their necks. Even though they have a foreign accent, you see other similarities between them and you: skin color, facial features, hair, the similar gestures. All these familiar things begin to make you feel related to them. You begin to feel identified with them. They are your people, your race, your religion. You see that one of "your" group is waving a large flag with the same symbol and you feel suddenly proud at seeing this flag with its safe and familiar symbol. You begin to be aware of your feelings watching these two groups of human beings. You feel anger and want to protect "your" group. You want to take sides. You feel threatened by this other group, this "enemy" to your group's way of life.

You watch all these feelings—the fear, the anger, the need to protect and defend "your group" against the "other," the "enemy." You are aware that you are reacting as if you are threatened physically, as if your actual survival is in jeopardy. Yet in truth, no one is physically threatening you.

You remember what your teachers at your school said to you before your trip. "Watch how you identify with certain people; see how that identification, that desire to be a part of the group, creates fears of being physically threatened even though it is not really happening." The students on this trip had talked all this over with their teachers before they left. This class trip was a very important part of their school studies in Human Relations. They were studying how their brains—the human brain—creates conflict in relationships through fear; how that fear creates a need to join a group for security and safety and how this then divided the human race into opposing groups and belief systems. The school is a special school—founded to understand the causes of conflict, and the extreme of conflict—war.

"Were you aware of what was happening to you?" a teacher asked that evening when all the students were back at the hotel. "Did you see how you were caught up in taking sides in that argument today? Why did it happen?"

"Because we have been conditioned to react in this way. For centuries this conditioning has been passed down, generation after generation to us. And we also believe, as our ancestors believed, that our particular way is the chosen way," one of the students responded to the teacher's question.

"And we still identify with our groups. And this creates conflict because we are separated, divided," another student spoke up.

"We felt threatened today, just as if we were in a dark alley with a dangerous person who was going to physically hurt us. Even though today there was no physical threat, I felt myself acting in the same way: my mouth got dry, my hands got wet, my heart sped up. I felt like I was preparing to fight or run away but there was no actual physical threat. I didn't know if it was a real or imaginary threat!" another student said.

"Why did you react to this argument as if it were a real threat to your physical well-being?" the teacher continued to question.

"I guess it was because I was identifying with one of the groups, with their symbols and with our similarities."

"Can you see now how what we call psychological conditioning—being caught up in identifying with a particular group, belief, or point of view—can cause you to feel physically threatened when your group, belief or point of view is being questioned or challenged?" the teacher continued.

"It's like having a war machine in our heads. Our brain has been conditioned to behave in a physically self-protective, defensive way to a psychological threat, so our body will actually react the same way under either condition. The war machine, our brain, is like a computer program that has malfunctioned. It thinks that there is a real threat when there is none. It's an illusion, a trick of the brain, a dream world of warriors, enemies, heroes and war. It's almost as if we were driven to go to war by this misunderstanding, this malfunction in our brains. This is not an intelligent way to act. It creates tremendous pain and suffering.

"We create conflict. Our brains malfunction because they link the *physical* need to defend with the *psychological*. When we identify ourselves with a group or an organized belief system, we experience great psychological and then physical conflict whenever the group or belief seems to be threatened. Understand this and you will bring about peace by seeing what has *prevented* it." One of the head teachers spoke with great intensity and urgency in her voice.

"This is real education: understanding relationships. Academics are important, but without a basic understanding of how we, in our brains, cause conflict, we will continue creating warriors to kill or be killed. A true and intelligent education will address these issues so you can live healthier, happier lives—without the terrible conflict of being a warrior."

The two small stories you just read show how human beings react to fear:

- biologically (physically)
- psychologically (mentally)

The automatic fight-or-flight mechanism for survival is designed for actual, physical threats—but we can react the same in both physically- *and* psychologically-threatening situations. Does all this seem hard for you to understand? If you keep at it you will begin to see how the human brain can be "programmed" to act like a war machine, how it creates tremendous conflict in relationships by a simple yet profound malfunction in the way it works.

Simply *seeing* how this malfunction operates begins to correct it. Conditioning *can* be changed through understanding, by seeing it as it occurs in us each moment. Understanding then changes our behavior—at the root, in our brain—so that outwardly we no longer create conflict.

How will you find out if all this is true? If you investigate like a good scientist, you will have a "working hypothesis." If you look at it like Sherlock Holmes, the clever detective, you have clues to deduce from. It's up to you. How will you begin your questioning?

?   ?   ?

Chapter 5

THE WARRIOR WAY OF LIFE

"I joined the Marines to be part of the few and the proud, to be able to defend our country, our democracy, our way of life from the forces of evil. I also wanted to obtain some type of skill to help me in my future career as a civilian. The military offered medical and dental benefits. It also offered the G.I. bill for college. These are some of the attractions that many young adults join the military for. During training I was taught to march like a soldier, how to treat my M-16 as my life, how to shoot and stab targets without fully realizing that these torn-up targets would one day be replaced by flesh and blood. My whole purpose in the Marines was to kill, to destroy, to annihilate anything out of existence. I was not conscious of it then, but I am now, and I do not wish to be part of the killing."

—*Sam Lwin, Conscientious Objector,*
Former Marine Corps Reservist,
October 1990*

*Reprinted with permission from *Fellowship of Reconciliation* newsletter, June 1991.

In 1990, the U. S. military spent over $2.4 billion ($2,400,000,000) to recruit over 300,000 young men and women into military service to become warriors. "Drafted" by the scarcity of civilian job opportunities and skyrocketing tuition, most young people join the military seeking job training and money for college. Those who fought in the Gulf War, however, learned that the military is not just about education, job skills or travel. Enlisting can also mean being ordered to kill.

Militarism is not just war. It is an attitude that glorifies weapons and emphasizes violent solutions to differences between people of different backgrounds and countries. Military recruiters, who are trained to sell you on joining, do not tell you about this attitude. As a result, many young students have joined in fear and confusion.

Whatever the military recruiters tell you about opportunities, once there is the possibility of war, the military is concerned with one thing: fighting and winning.

Recruiting Warriors—Advertising

Perhaps you've heard a recruiter's sales pitch—travel, training, money for college. "Be all that you can be." "We're looking for a few good men." "The few, the proud, the Marines." Sound good, don't they? They present the military as a fulfilling, elite club, while accompanying messages stress the education, job training, travel and financial benefits of service. Advertisements featuring soldiers zipping down ropes hung from helicopters or crossing flimsy suspension bridges make the military look enjoyable and thrilling—a lot like a wilderness adventure camp. The ads rarely mention weapons and almost

77

never raise the possibility of combat or war.

Science and Engineering

The Armed Forces get many recruits by promising them exciting work in science and engineering. What they mean by science and engineering is: missile technology, gun sights, bomb sights, radar, atomic bombs, and chemical and biological warfare—all of which have the capability of annihilating the world.

School Access

The military maintains almost 15,000 full-time recruiters nationwide (more than $200 million per year in salaries). While searching out eligible seventeen- and eighteen-year-olds, these recruiters enlist the cooperation of educators and administrators to gain access to high schools. Many high schools allow recruiters regular access to students in their hallways, and even allow them to use guidance counselor offices to speak to potential recruits. Some schools allow the military to bring in tanks, helicopters or guns onto school property for show.

Recruiters also regularly seek student directory information from schools to aid their efforts. After obtaining student names, addresses and home phone numbers, recruiters will often contact students repeatedly by phone, seeking appointments. Some young people receive up to ten calls from a single branch of the military.

Publications

The Pentagon currently sends 19,000,000 pieces of bulk mail to the homes of sixteen- to twenty-one-year-olds every year. The military uses many different mailing lists, from "teen" magazines to motor vehicle ownership records. The mailings often offer a free gift (sweat socks, posters, etc.) for returning a postage-paid card. Every year, these mailings produce a half million "leads" for local recruiters. Every fall, *Futures,* a full-color magazine published for the military by Scholastic Magazine, is mailed free to three million high school seniors, featuring short articles on vocational and career issues, along with numerous recruiting ads.

If you think you want to join the military, to become a warrior, you'll be making a decision that will change your life. Before you do, know what you are getting into.

✦ Talk to people who have been in the military and liked it. Why did they?

✦ Talk to people who have been in the military and did not like it. Why didn't they?

✦ Read. Ask questions. Do your own thinking.

The Warrior Way of Life

The military offers jobs and educational opportunities, but there's more than that. The General Accounting Office (GAO) said in 1986:

"The basic purpose of military forces—to engage in combat when called upon—requires that an individual respond immediately and without question to an order to put his/her life on the line. This principle of obedience permeates the entire military establishment, placing the individual wholly at the disposal of the organization."

Being a warrior is not just a job. It's a way of life. And it has *complete* control over yours!

You Are Not Your Own Master

Once you join the military:

✦ You cannot just quit if you find that the military is not for you.

✦ You can request a discharge for medical problems, but there is no guarantee that the military will grant your request.

✦ You must place the needs of the military above your own. The military can, for example, move you across the country or the world—regardless of the problems this creates for you.

✦ You are subject to the Uniform Code of Military Justice, a set of military laws that includes crimes

80

which would not be crimes in civilian life. For instance, you can be court-martialed (and then punished) for "neglect of duty," insubordination (disobedience), or leaving the military without permission. The military court can impose punishments ranging from loss of pay, loss of rank, bad-conduct discharges to imprisonment and even—for desertion or treason—the *death penalty*.

You Lose a Lot of Rights

Here are some of the things the military can do that a civilian employer cannot:

➤ The military can legally limit your freedom of speech.

➤ The military can subject you to what in civilian life would be "unreasonable searches and seizures" of your personal property.

➤ You will have no right to sue the government for injuries you receive in the line of duty, racial discrimination, discrimination on the basis of sex, or intentional violation of your constitutional rights.

➤ You will not be permitted to join unions or engage in collective bargaining of any kind to improve your working conditions.

You May Not Get the Training or Job You Want

✈ Many recruits get the training and job they want, but a great many do not. Military training is for military jobs, not for a civilian job when you get out.

✈ The military is not really a school or job training center. It's a fighting force. It trains people in skills that will be useful to a fighting force.

✈ The enlistment agreement says that what's written in it is "all the promises made to me by the Government. Anything else anyone has promised me is not valid and will not be honored." This even includes promises from *recruiters*.

✈ Unemployment among young veterans is about 35% *higher* than among non-veterans of the same age.

✈ The enlistment contract says your status, pay, benefits and responsibilities in the military can change without warning, regardless of any promises in your contract.

The Hardest Issue of All

When you join the military, you are saying that you are willing to be part of war. That's a harder decision than you may think. Being a part of war means that you are willing to kill and die when someone else orders you to do so. It means you are willing to go anywhere the government says you should go to fight anybody the government says is your enemy. This could mean orders to bomb villages where there might be children. It could mean being ready to launch a nuclear missile that would turn a whole city into radioactive ashes in seconds.

Chapter 6

PATRIOTISM—THE ENEMY OF PEACE?

In order to understand why people act as warriors, as we did when we looked at how warriors create heroes, we need to look at a very important and "touchy" subject—patriotism.

What Is Patriotism?

I looked up the meaning of "patriot" in the American College Dictionary. Here is what it says:

Patriot: a person who loves and loyally or zealously supports his or her own country

Every country has its patriots—people who love their country so much that they would give their own lives to support and defend it. Such devotion has come about through centuries of conditioned tribal belief systems, beliefs that separate people into opposing factions; therefore it's important for you to know that it can be dangerous. The key word in the definition of patriot is "zealously." A zealot can be someone who wears blinders—who does not see the whole picture and does not ask questions to uncover the whole truth.

A good example of "patriotism" could be seen in the war with Iraq. During the days of Desert Storm, people worldwide, especially in America, were all bombarded with television ads, posters, signs on buildings and in streets, magazine stories, and newspaper headlines about the fight for what was "good" and "right." People were bathed in nationalism—taking great pride in their nation, right or wrong. Many schools supported the war effort, piping in bugle music, and writing letters to the troops. Desert Storm buttons and T-shirts were worn by students and teachers. Patriotism was viewed as strong support for the war, the selling of war toys, and the glamorizing of weapons of destruction. Do you remember hearing of the "success" of weapons called "Patriot Missiles"? Did this make you feel proud?

Warriors and people who thought that the only way to solve the problem was through violence supported war in the Middle East. They felt they were being patriotic, good citizens by protecting the "free" world from the enemy. But this form of patriotism doesn't solve the problem. It only makes things worse because it still keeps people apart! Patriotism has a larger meaning than fighting a war for one's country:

Patriotism goes beyond support for a war. Patriotism can also be *opposition to* war.

Many people passionately, fundamentally do not believe in war—any war—because it is terribly destructive. These people, and I am among them, do not see war as an honorable and successful venture. It is a monstrously insane act that we have come to think of as a rational, necessary and even honorable way to bring about peace!

A New Patriotism

Can patriotism be looked at in a new, more intelligent way, a way that supports the entire human race rather than a separate, divided tribe, race or country? This means that if you think our *world* will be harmed by war, you have the right to say so and ought to say so. When you think intelligently, you can act intelligently and for the whole of humanity instead of for a particular nationalistic, racial or religious belief system.

Questions:

1. Can a person prevent peace worldwide by being fanatically loyal to his or her country?

2. Do you remember when we talked about early humans joining tribes and how this created conflict between the tribes and created "the enemy"?

3. Is a country's patriotism similar to the belief of long-ago tribes that their way was the only way?

4. Can a patriot possibly create separation, and therefore prevent peace, between human beings by being a patriot? How?

5. Can we be against a war, or war in general, and still be patriotic?

6. Do you think we could be patriotic about the *world*?

Patriotism for a particular country is a threat
to the Earth.
It divides the Earth into parts
and separates human beings from one another.

7. To be patriotic about the world, would we have to outlaw war, pollution and anything that threatens our planet?

8. Do you think being patriotic about the world is more beneficial than being patriotic about one's country? Why?

9. If we go on defending only our own group, race, religion or country, will we continue to create greater and greater separation, division and conflict—and, therefore, more war?

10. Can we stop being part of a separate tribe, nation, race, or organized belief system and therefore relate to the whole—be a member of the *Human Race*? How might this end global conflict?

Chapter 7

THE HOLY WARRIORS

To Die a Glorious Death

They could hear the enemy coming through the thick jungle. They could smell the terrible odor of fear. They gripped their automatic rifles. They were very alert to all movements. Suddenly the enemy stood up and moved forward. There were three of them, adults in combat uniforms. The young boys stood up, fired rapid, jerking bursts of gun fire, and the three adults fell like dead weights into the tall grass.

The three boys, ages eleven, twelve and thirteen, went over to the dead, bleeding figures. One of the adults had been hit in the face; part of his skull was missing. Blood covered his face, hair and chest. The other two adults were bleeding profusely, dark holes in their uniforms where the crashing bullets entered. The boys thumped the bodies of the adults with their rifle butts to make sure they were dead. The boys had killed often. They had been warriors since they were nine years old. Now it was all business—the business of killing.

"How did it feel, boy?" the adult commander asked one of them.

"I was happy because I killed them," he answered slowly, deliberately. "I enjoyed myself. It was exciting. Now I will live in our holy land forever after."

"And you," the commander looked coldly at one of the

other boys.

"I kill because either we kill them or they will kill us. If they die a glorious death according to their religion, they will die in honor. But I must kill for our honor, for my people, my beliefs. It is an honor to die for my beliefs. I will not let the enemy's foot into my country. He is an infidel," the boy answered in a well-practiced chant, memorized from their classes.

The next night the three boys captured four enemy soldiers. They tied the prisoners' hands, blindfolded them and marched them back to their camp. After their commander spoke to the prisoners, the boys lined the prisoners up and shot them.

Every day, except once a week, the boys go to their lessons. They each have automatic rifles. They also are trained to handle bigger weapons, like rocket launchers and bazookas. Over the years, they are indoctrinated into the lessons of Holy War. Their school is a dark, windowless concrete room with military pictures and slogans on the walls. The little academics they get are mixed with their religious beliefs. An algebra problem shows that their God is one. History is taught to demonstrate that their religion is the oldest, the chosen one to which God gave special rights—to save the world by ridding it of the "unclean ones," the defilers, the heathens, their enemies. They call it "religious cleansing," which means torture, murder and mass killings of anyone who doesn't believe in their chosen way.

"Who is ready to fight?" the teacher calls out to the young boys.

A six-year old boy, small but fierce, stands up and recites the well-rehearsed chant.

"I will honor my God; to die for him is an honor. Death to those who don't believe!" He salutes and then sits down smiling. The teacher does not smile. This is serious business.

In the afternoon the boys practice skills, pretending to step around an imaginary minefield filled with deadly disk-shaped explosive devices.

That next night the three boys are given the real task of detecting the mines—a job of great honor. Pinning pictures of their religious leader on the boys' shirts, the adult commander orders them forward. It has to be done in order to advance the soldiers. Hundreds of young boys before them sacrificed life and limb for the glory of their leader and religion. For this is a Holy War, a war to end all war, a war of peace, to save humans from their sins, to bring their religion to the unfaithful. To die in battle is the highest glory.

It is a moonless night. The jungle seems endless. The enemy could be anywhere. Under the silent cover of darkness the three boys creep forward, feeling the ground with long sticks like blind men, searching for land mines to dig up and make harmless.

Ever so slowly, sweat dripping from their bodies, their eyes straining intensely, their hearts beating fiercely in their chests, they move forward with infinite caution. "Your leader will honor you. Your God will give you life everlasting. There is no greater glory than to serve and die for them," they could hear their teacher tell them in a mechanical, hard, practiced

92

manner. These words give them courage to move forward into this terrible danger. And because they trust the adults and want their approval, these young boys go out in that minefield to clear the way for the regular adult soldiers in their drive to conquer the enemy of their religion.

It happened, as tragedy does, in an unexpected, sudden moment. The sound and flash sent them all flying up and backwards, with smoking dirt.

They woke up in the dingy hospital, lying face up on stretchers. One boy's wrists were tied to the bedpost in order to prevent him from ripping off his bandages. The second boy lay on his side. He slowly came to and blinked at the bright, dirty lights glaring down at him from the ceiling. He was completely numb. He could move only one arm. He felt bandages on his stomach and then lower on his legs. He felt a strange painful feeling in his legs, an awful aching sensation. He felt he could move his toes and was suddenly relieved. He reached down to rub his right leg and found only emptiness. He reached quickly for his left leg and there too found emptiness. His legs felt as if they were tucked up under him so he reached behind him, but still there was only emptiness. He leaned up a bit and looked down at his lower body. What was once his legs were now bloody bandaged stumps. His legs were gone, from the thighs down.

In nearby beds, young boys all around them were moaning and calling out pitifully. "The pain! The pain!" The boys were given morphine to kill the pain. Young boys called for their mothers.

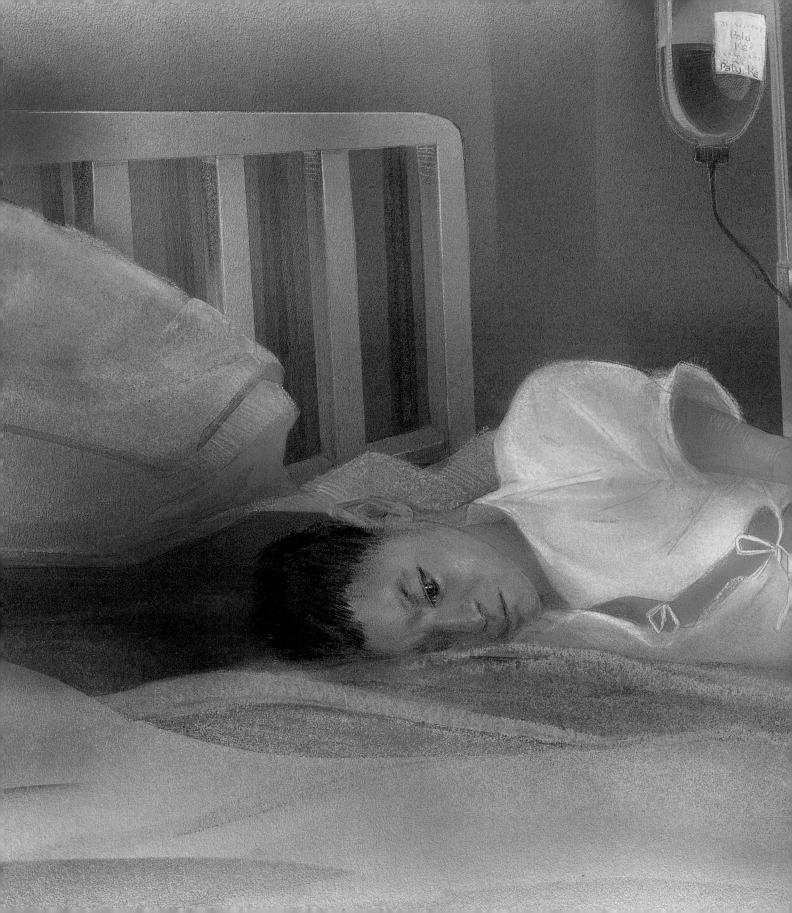

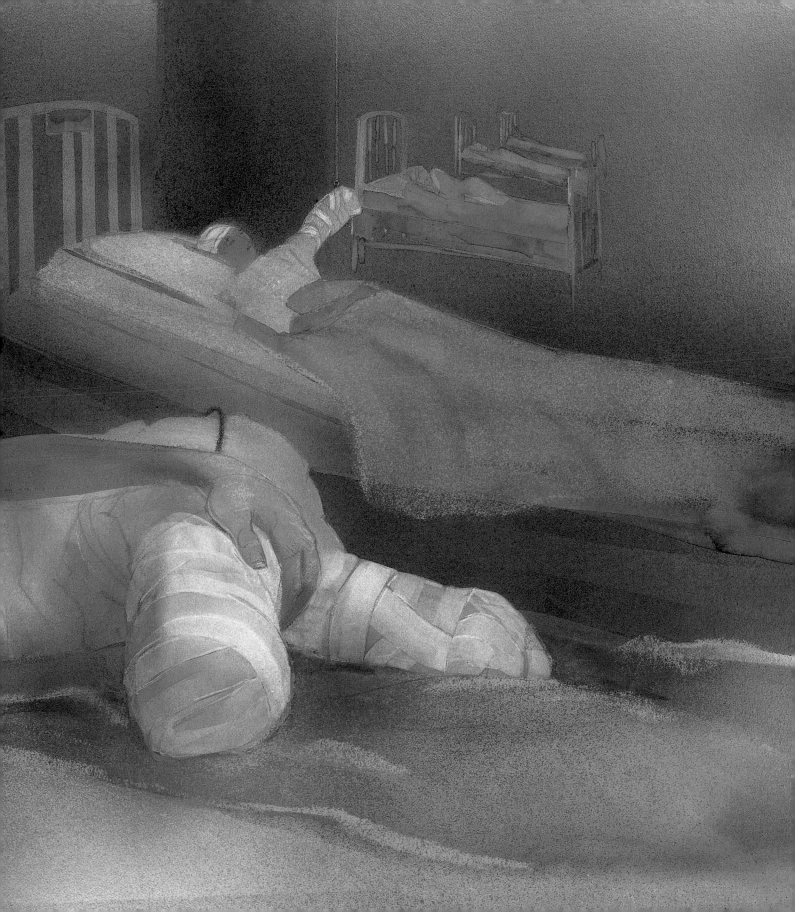

The third boy on the night in the minefield had been blown to bits. He stepped directly on a very large land mine. There was nothing left.

One of the boys in a bed nearby cried out, "I must die for honor, my God will give me eternal life. I will fight again to kill the enemy or be killed. It is our way. It has always been our way."

On the wall, a torn, soiled banner reads: "Death before Dishonor!" In the distance new young recruits are singing the Holy Warrior's fighting song:

"Onward Holy Soldiers, marching out to war,
   Our mighty fortress is our God,
   Praise to his wondrous warrior spirit,
   His shield of truth and righteousness,
   Shall save us one and all."

Children Conditioned to Fight for Peace

The story you've just read is true. It has happened thousands of times before. Today as you read these words, young people are being conditioned to "fight for peace," for their religious beliefs. In Northern Ireland, in Cambodia, Thailand, in Afghanistan, in Africa, *children* are being trained as soldiers—Holy Warriors—to defend the beliefs of their religious and political leaders. It is estimated that more than *200,000* children under the age of fifteen are being trained today in armies around the world.

Thousand of children are killing and being killed! Children as young as eight years old are fighting adult enemies they don't know, for reasons they don't understand. *And for what?*

Religious or Holy Wars have been fought for thousands of years all over our earth by differing religious belief systems.

During the Crusades in the 12th and 13th centuries, thousands of young men volunteered to fight for the freedom of the holy places in Palestine to get control from the Muslims and establish and maintain Christian control there. As Crusaders, they were to stitch red crosses on their cloaks to show they were soldiers of Christ. A major reason these young men went to join in the war, to kill and be killed, was the church promised them a "full indulgence"—that is, full forgiveness of all their sins and a promise that they would enter heaven directly when they died in battle.

The Middle East has been a religious battleground for centuries with many religious belief systems fighting for control. The constant struggle between the Arabs and the Israelis has been a horrifying example of what can happen when people of the same lands and race are divided by belief systems. This is also true of the continuous bloody battles between the Protestants and Catholics in Northern Ireland. The history of humankind has witnessed the slaughter of millions of human beings in the name of God, righteousness and glory.

Religion, an Organized Belief System

People who are drawn to religious life are gentle, fine, peaceful people who sense that there is more to the world than material gain—money, fame, possessions and power. They feel a need for "God," something "spiritual" or "divine." I too have felt this yearning for a spiritual life. As a young man I was attracted to becoming a monk and living a life dedicated to religious peace and harmony. I still feel this way. Some of this yearning is genuine, and yet I think it can also be an attempt to escape from the harshness of life, to go back to childhood when I felt protected and innocent. Hiding or going back to the past is not the answer.

All of us have a yearning for something spiritual in our lives, and since religion professes to bring peace, many of us turn to religion to find that peace. But to live a holy, religious, peaceful or spiritual life, we must actively understand what *prevents* us from living a peaceful life. Being religious or peaceful cannot come about by wishful thinking, hope or faith. Peace comes about when we can look at and understand the fears, greed, ambition and violence in ourselves and those around us. When you can understand what makes you *not* peaceful, then you can understand the cause of war, whether a personal war or a global war. Whether there is conflict with a bully on a playground or conflict with a bullying nation that wants to harm other people, what is happening is war. War is war!

It is important to question how religion, which professes to give us peace, can create so many holy warriors, to question the sanity of turning eight-year-old children into killers or putting them in positions dangerous enough to kill them. In the Children's Crusade of the 13th Century, thousands of children went to the Holy Land from Europe to "fight" the enemy. These children were unarmed and undefended; their very youth was meant to frighten the enemy, making it difficult for these enemies to destroy them. Most of the children died of starvation or disease along the way, or were captured by pirates and made into slaves. Do you see anything peaceful about this?

Please see that I am not condemning religions or religious leaders—of any kind. I only want to understand how established belief systems separate people and create conflict. Religion is an organized belief system, a way of thinking and acting according to a particular cultural, racial or national bias—a set of ideals by which we believe we should live. These ideals come from hundreds of generations passing their beliefs down to new generations—beliefs formed in early tribal groups to explain the unknown and make everyone feel more secure. In gaining this false sense of security, people lost their larger sense of togetherness; their opposing beliefs put them into deep conflict.

As you look with new eyes at yourself and the world around you, see whether this is true—that established ideals and beliefs separate people and create conflict. If so, then you have discovered the source of conflict, war, and our need for warriors. In this self-questioning, you are using your brain and expanding your mental power. It is this questioning, this new intelligence that is awakening, that will create real peace and a truly spiritual, holy, religious life.

Questions:

1. How can people have *Holy* Wars?

2. Is there anything holy about war?

3. Is there anything in being holy that creates war?

4. Is the human race divided by established religious beliefs, separated into different ways of living? Can this cause conflict between us?

5. How has religion been used to promote war?

6. Can one be religious and at the same time advocate war?

7. Are there religions whose people work for peace? Do they achieve peace? What do they do?

8. Is living a religious life different than following a religion? How?

9. In order to be peaceful or holy, does a person need to believe in a particular religious system? Why?

10. Do you think there is a religious way of life that can end war? How?

Chapter 8

PARENTS—RAISING WARRIORS?

Most parents love and care for their children; they want them to live healthy and happy lives. So why do so many parents send their children off to war to kill and be killed? It doesn't make sense! But if you see that parents have been deeply conditioned to believe that the way to solve problems between people is through war and have been "brainwashed" to think that their own country, nation, race, or religion must be defended, protected—then you can understand why they send their children off to the military, and often to war.

Conditioning is so strong that people will sacrifice themselves, their children, homes and cities in the name of honor, pride, patriotism—that is, for an ideal, an image of what they have been told to believe is good, right and honorable. This is an incredibly sad and tragic thing! Fortunately there are more and more parents who recognize what conditioning is: they intelligently question blind allegiance to a particular tribe (country/nation/race) and educate their children to resolve the challenges of human relationship through creative, *non*violent means. These families don't accept that war is inevitable or that we have to violently defend a piece of earth (tribal territory) to the death for some "honorable" ideal. They recognize that nationalistic and racial ideals are destructive, and as citizens of the earth, they honor an undivided world—a "global community."

It is not for us to judge or condemn those parents—fathers and mothers who are deeply conditioned to believe in "nationalism" and "racism" and will defend against an "enemy" by sacrificing their children to their particular ideal. We can only look at what is actually happening, question any conditioning before it takes hold, and do our best to prevent ourselves and others from acting blindly in defense of some cause.

Fathers—Raising Warriors

Men constitute the majority of warriors today and in the past. Let's look first at how men as fathers have been an influence in the creation of warriors. The best way to look at what we believe is to ask ourselves questions.

Think about these questions:

— Do you think men are born with more aggression than women? Are men more easily turned into warriors?
— Are young boys turned into warriors when they start to play at war?
— When a father says to his son, "Be a man!" what does he mean?
— In what competitive activities do males typically participate that might promote warlike behavior?

— What "manly" images does the media present to boys?
— How is a boy raised to treat other boys?
— How is a boy raised to treat girls?
— What pressure are fathers under to have their sons be warriors?
— Would a son who refused to be a warrior be looked on as a coward, a deserter, a failure in the eyes of his community, his country, his race?

Mothers—Raising Warriors

Many people believe that only men are violent and warlike. They believe that women, especially mothers, have little or nothing to do with their sons (and now daughters) becoming warriors. Is this true? Let's look at this role mothers play in raising warriors and consider more questions:

— Do mothers encourage their sons to fight for their country? If so, how?
— Does such encouragement start with wanting him to win, to be successful, to be a "man," the protector of the homeland, race and nation?
— How does a mother's image of herself as a "good" mother, bringing up a "good" son, enter into her thinking? Is her image of a "good" son one who would be willing to give up his life for his country, his race?
— Is a mother afraid that she and her family will be outcasts from society if they don't conform in this way?

103

— How do caring mothers send their children off to kill men, women, children, and destroy homes, cities, countries—or to die a horrible death?

— Some people think that if the world were run by women, there would be no more wars. What do you think about this?

— Are women more naturally gentle than men?

— Do women contribute to making a warrior?

— Is a military man in uniform appealing to women? Does this encourage men to join the military?

— Do women now want to be like men and also "fight for peace"? In some countries women can join or are forced to join the military. Although women are now more actively engaged in the military, they usually hold noncombat positions.

It is important, in trying to find out what creates a warrior, *not to* judge or blame any person, any group of people, any country or race. Blame is destructive for it only breeds hate—not understanding. And it is understanding— seeing the truth of what is actually happening— that will free us!

Is this a fact or a belief?
How will you find out?
By questioning?

WHAT ARE THE EFFECTS OF BEING A WARRIOR?

Chapter 9

ONE ATOMIC BOMB

It is common for us to hear about it when a country is building atomic bombs or increasing its supply of them. We barely look up in surprise when television news broadcasts make the announcement. We have been conditioned to think of an atomic bomb as a weapon of defense—something we need to represent our strength.

Because it is a monstrously destructive weapon, it is necessary for you to know exactly what would happen if *one* atomic bomb hit your town today. There is a good chance no one has ever described this to you. In order to understand war in this day and age, it is essential that you really understand what this means—not on television, but actually. Please understand that the reason the description is so graphic is because every word is true, and I want you to understand the truth. I don't want to frighten you but to wake you up to what is real. Being a warrior means being trained to kill other human beings. Perhaps after reading this you will think twice about wanting to be a warrior—you will see that it is not a child's game—it is also not an "adventure," a "challenge," or a "rewarding job," as the military might want you to think.

✈ In the first few milliseconds of the dropping of an atomic bomb in your town, you see an enormously blinding light, as if the sun were a few hundred yards away—brighter than any light you could ever see or imagine.

✈   A second later, a great heat forms a fireball, like a gigantic blowtorch that reaches seventeen to thirty million degrees Fahrenheit, vaporizing everything in a circle about a half mile in all directions from the center. People are reduced to ashes instantly, leaving only shadows on the ground. Your friends, family, school, home, are gone in an instant—in the most horrifying way ever imagined.

✈   Two seconds after the explosion, four miles from the explosion, everything turns to fire.

✈   Four to five seconds later, a great blast, as if the sky itself is landing with unimaginable force, crushes you on the ground with winds starting at 500-700 miles per hour. At a distance of six to seven miles from the center (Ground Zero), a person standing in his or her living room looking through a closed window towards the flash of light will suddenly experience these windows turning into a wave of thousands of pieces of glass, traveling hundreds of miles per hour, shredding anything or anyone in its path.

✈   Ten to sixty minutes after the blast, widespread fires blaze from the intense heat, exploding gas stations, collapsing buildings, burning the countryside to a crisp. A huge mushroom cloud rises up like a gigantic tornado, sucking into it human ashes, the dust that was once men, women and children.

110

✦ Two hours after the blast, mortally wounded people stagger around in shock. All medical aid is destroyed and hospitals are in flames. There is no electricity or water. Civilization as we know it is gone. Cities and towns are reduced to nothing.

✦ Twelve hours after the blast, massive numbers of people die. Blast shelters have become crematoriums, people in them roasted alive or crushed or choked to death. Radioactive dust settles, drifting down from the mushroom cloud, continuing to kill people for *years*.

✦ Days and weeks later, people who survived the blast are now dying from wounds, infections, psychological stress. Robberies, murders, and cannibalism are committed at random by people who are trying to stay alive at all costs.

What you have read, just a small sample of what could happen, *has* happened. It happened at Nagasaki and Hiroshima in Japan during the Second World War when bombs were dropped on both those cities. If it happened once, it could happen again.

There are over *60,000* nuclear warheads active today that could wipe out every man, woman and child *twenty times over*. Biological warfare, which uses micro-organisms as disease germs to destroy humans, animals and plants, could do the same. Why?

Think a moment about how angry, frightened or filled with hate one country, one group of people, would have to be to cause this kind of death and destruction. Think beyond the hatred, fear and anger about the men, women and children who would perish, the land that would be destroyed, the years of poisonous air and the disappearance of everything cherished.

We Are the War

Wars are started not by "bad," evil human beings, but by people like you and me. *We are the war.* Why do we start wars? Because we have been conditioned to think and act in certain ways that create war:

○ We create differences between ourselves and others.

○ We see other people as "enemies."

○ We are trained to believe that war is common and necessary—and even heroic.

○ We are taught to believe that we, the average person, can do nothing about war, that only the "experts" or "authorities" can solve our problems of relationship.

○ We believe that in our violent world, individuals have little or no effect, that only governments or large political groups have power to change our lives.

112

(Did you notice that even using "we," "they," and "other" in the above sentences divides the whole human race into parts or fragments? Can you see that the very language we use is also conditioned to create separations? How we think creates how we act.)

> ## The truth is that *we* are the world and the world is us.

Questions:

1. What did you feel when you read the account of the bomb?

2. Does this information make you feel afraid? Hopeless? Confused?

3. Do you think this devastation might have been prevented?

4. Do you think people should have done something to prevent this? If yes, what?

5. Why do you think people drop bombs on people?

6. Who starts war? And why?

7. Do *you* ever create war? At home? At school?

8. How do you create war?

9. Have you ever felt like a warrior? When?

10. What turned you into a warrior?

11. Have you ever helped solve a problem peacefully that could've erupted into a "war?" When?

Chapter 10

THE COST OF WAR

"It will be a great day when our day care centers have all the money they need and the Navy has to hold a bake sale to buy battleships."

— War Resisters League

Dear Reader—

I have written the following so you will have some idea what war costs—not only in the loss of human life, but in resources that—if put to other, more humane uses—could solve so many human problems. If you are young and have not had life experiences that help you understand everything in this book, I want you to know that what is important is to open your mind and simply imagine the new concepts that this book offers you. What's important is to see, beyond your fear, the need to change how human beings relate to each other. It's a fact that there have only been about 300 years during the past 5,000 when people have *not* been at war somewhere in the world. We must find a way to stop this seemingly endless cycle of violence.

You may think, "Who am I? I can't change the world. It's up to the politicians, the generals, the leaders. I'm nobody!" You are not the first person to have these thoughts. We have all been conditioned to think this way. But it's time for you to

see that this is not intelligent, responsible thinking. *You* are the world! There is no world separate from you! If *you* stop war in your mind, if *you* recognize that being a warrior is destructive and cannot bring about peace, then *you* are playing a part in ending war! If every person does the same, war is over!

Some people believe that understanding war is complicated, and that a young person like you cannot understand it like the "authorities" do. *Please question* people who say this! Find out for yourself what is true! In your life, you create conflict. You can resolve your conflict by becoming responsible for it and looking at the way you think and act.

The Cost of Past Wars in Human Lives (1900 - 1993)

Over *150 million* human beings have been killed between 1900 and 1993 in war. That is well over one million per year! Imagine if 150 million people suddenly disappeared from the United States: *two out of every three* men, women and children throughout the country would vanish. The list below shows *just a few* of the countless wars and conflicts in modern history, and how many soldiers died in them. Killings of civilians—men, women and children who are not soldiers—add millions more to the total cost in human life. In fact, since 1945, more civilians than soldiers have been killed during wartime—a total of more than twenty million innocent people dead and sixty million wounded. Eighty percent of these civilian casualties were women and children.

War	People Killed
World War I	19,600,000
World War II	38,400,000*
Vietnam	2,958,000
Korea	2,889,000
Cambodia	2,156,000
China	2,000,000
Nigeria	2,000,000
Persian Gulf War	100,000**

*Almost 500,000 (1/2 million) civilians were killed when *one* atomic bomb consisting of approximately 1.5 megatons was dropped on Japan. Estimates of total military and civilian deaths resulting from World War II range as high as 60,000,000 (sixty million).

**All these Persian Gulf deaths occured during a war lasting *less than six weeks.*

> **We now have atomic bombs worldwide totalling in excess of 18,000 megatons, which is the equivalent of 6,000 World War IIs.**

Two of the most murderous dictators in modern times—Adolf Hitler and Josef Stalin—are examples of how much violence, suffering and terror can be brought about just by the beliefs and actions of an individual human being. Under Hitler's direction, Nazis put to death 6,000,000 (*six million*) innocent Jewish civilians, as well as hundreds of thousands of Poles and Russians—not to mention enemy soldiers. During his "Great Terror," Stalin kept power by ordering the shooting or imprisonment and torture of countless Russian citizens. He was responsible for about 10,000,000 (*ten million*) deaths of his own citizens, and if you add the military deaths during his rule, and civilian war deaths from air raids and famine, the number climbs to *twenty million deaths.*

The Cost of Present War Planning in U. S. Dollars

In addition to human lives, war costs an almost unbelievable amount of money. The United States *alone* will spend over $3,000,000,000,000 (three trillion dollars) in just ten years, planning for war. Can you conceive of how much three trillion dollars is? It is three million dollars a day for the next 2,730 *years.* If you counted out three trillion one dollar bills at the rate of one bill every second, twenty-four hours per day, it would take 96,000 *years.*

Three trillion dollars could buy a $300,000 furnished house for *every family* in Kansas, Missouri, Nebraska, Oklahoma and Iowa. Then you could put a $30,000 car in the garage of each house. There would still be money left to build ten new $3 million libraries and ten new $3 million hospitals in each of 250 cities, and there would *still* be enough money left to build ten $3 million schools for 500 communities.

Would you believe that there would still be enough money left in the bank to pay the salaries of 10,000 nurses and teachers just from the interest alone, plus give a $15,000 bonus to every family in those states each year—*forever*?

Only ten percent (10%) of the $3 trillion spent could solve the following human and environmental problems:

119

Problems on Earth	Cost of Repair
Stop ozone depletion	$ 5.0 billion
Eliminate illiteracy	5.0 billion
Stop deforestation	7.0 billion
Prevent global warming	8.0 billion
Prevent acid rain	8.0 billion
Stabilize population	10.5 billion
Provide health care	15.0 billion
Eliminate starvation/malnourishment	19.0 billion
Provide shelter	21.0 billion
Prevent soil erosion	24.0 billion
Retire developing nations' debts	30.0 billion
Provide efficient renewable energy	50.0 billion
Provide safe, clean water	50.0 billion

Did you know:

+ One modern fighter plane can cost $50 million to build?

+ Five percent (5%) of the military budget could take *every* child out of poverty?

+ The U.S. Army spends over $6,000 just to attract and recruit *one* new soldier?

DID SPEND FOR MILITARY:	COULD SPEND FOR HUMANITY
• Trident II submarine and fighter plane program: **$100 billion**	• Cleanup of 10,000 worst U.S. toxic waste dumps: **$100 billion**
• 1991 research of SDI, the "Star Wars" program: **$2.5 billion**	• Cost of fully immunizing 33 million children: **$2.5 billion**
• Money paid to top five military contractors in 1989: **$28.5 billion**	• Annual cost of eliminating all poverty in the U.S.: **$26.7 billion**
• One B-2 "Stealth" bomber: **$530 million**	• One day's approximate interest on U.S. national debt: **$500 million**
• One U.S. nuclear test: **$12 million**	• Cost to train 40,000 health workers in Third World: **$12 million**
• Cost of creating 75,700 jobs by military spending: **$1 billion**	• Cost of creating 139,000 jobs by health spending: **$1 billion**
• One year research, Midgetman and MX missiles: **$680 million**	• Medicare for all poor and near-poor families: **$500 million**
• Two days of global military spending: **$4.8 billion**	• Annual cost to halt Third World desertification: **$4.8 billion**
• Three days of global military spending: **$6.5 billion**	• Five years of funding the UN Tropical Forest plan: **$6.5 billion**
• Two weeks of global military spending: **$30 billion**	• Annual cost of UN Water and Sanitation Decade: **$30 billion**

✈   The entire budget for the Peace Corps is less than
     what the U.S. military spends on its marching bands?

Who do you think pays the bill for this incredible spending? You may be surprised to discover we all do, including your parents, teachers and your adult friends. When you are earning a living, you will be paying for it, too. Everyone is required by law to pay taxes to the government from the money made in daily work. The government spends *huge* amounts of this money on weapons and the military. You and I have been conditioned to believe this spending is necessary, even beneficial.

**Who is directly or indirectly responsible
for the proliferation of weapons in preparation of war?
You and I.
Why?
Because we cannot resolve our day-to-day conflicts,
conflicts that lead to war!**

**The Cost of Future Wars
in U. S. Dollars**

The cost of human life in future wars is frightening to ponder. It is difficult to imagine that there would be any life left on the planet at all. Yet the United States government continues to spend money developing weapons that are capable of destroying every living thing on earth. (Please note: I am using the United States only as one example among many governments that are doing the same thing.)

122

Every *minute* 30 children die of hunger and inadequate health care, while the world spends $1,700,000 on war.

Questions:

1. Did you know that this much money was being spent on war?

2. What do you think about this spending?

3. Do you think that millions of human lives could be saved if we had the right kind of education, an education that taught people how to resolve human conflict peacefully?

4. If it were up to you to spend $1 million today on something beneficial for people, what would you spend the money on?

5. If it were up to you to spend $5 million today on something beneficial for our planet, what would you spend the money on?

6. If you were the leader of a country, what would you do to end this terrible cost of human lives and resources?

7. What can you do as a young person to help stop this waste?

8. Why have we accepted this?

9. Do you feel overwhelmed by all these numbers?

10. Can you see that it all starts with each person and that if each of us refused to spend our hard-earned living on the destruction of human life that there would be no money to support war?

11. Did you know that today, if a person refuses to pay the portion of their taxes used to fund war, they can be fined or imprisoned?

12. Do you think the government needs an alternative "Peace Tax Fund" for people opposed to war? If so, what should it be used for?

✪ ✪ ✪

DID YOU KNOW?
The Impact of "Local Conflicts" on Children in the *Last Ten Years!*

✈ 1.5 million children have been killed.
✈ 4 million children have been physically disabled by land mines, firearms, torture, etc.
✈ 5 million children are in refugee camps.
✈ 12 million children have lost their homes.
✈ Whole generations have lost years of schooling.
✈ Countless children are orphaned or abandoned.

Chapter 11

IF YOU BELIEVE IN PEACE, WHY PLAY AT WAR?

Dear Reader—

If you no longer play with war toys, then this section will not directly relate to you. But it is still important because you can help younger kids who do. If you have younger brothers or sisters, you can help them by reading over this section together. Or you can talk it over with adults who parent or teach younger children. Warriors start being warriors when playing at war!

A company* that makes badges and bumper stickers has come out with a sticker it would like to see on all war toys. This is what it says:

> **WARNING:**
> **Think before you buy. This is a war toy. Playing with it increases anger and violence in children. Is this what you _really_ want for your child?**

* Donnelly/Colt, Inc., PO Box 188, Hampton, CT 06247, USA

Toy gun and weapon sales have risen dramatically in the past several years. Can you guess why? They are sold with a variety of gimmicks to make them more realistic and exciting:

✦ Motorized water guns "look and sound like the real thing—fire water blasts up to 30 times before re-loading," says the ad.

✦ Guns fire red pellets that are meant to look like blood stains when the opponent is hit. (A popular version of this gun has a warning that it should not be used by children under 16, yet it's sold in toy sections.)

✦ Laser guns, which fire a light that has been mistaken by police for gunfire, come with a target that reacts to the "laser" and can be worn by the opponent or hung for target practice.

✦ Realistically-detailed toy Israeli Uzi submachine guns are now made by many companies.

Toy companies know that when there is a war going on, playing with realistic toy guns is exciting to children. There are two different beliefs about the effects these toys can have on children. Some people say that war toys do nothing but teach children to be aggressive, violent and less sensitive to other people's thoughts and feelings. Others say war toys are part of "fantasy play" and help a child release aggression. What is the truth?

Here is something to think about:

Five out of six of the best-selling toys in the U.S. are war toys. According to the National Coalition against TV Violence, sales of these toys have increased 350% in the last two years, with 60% of the money spent on toys now going for guns and other toys of aggression.

A toy of violence is a toy that:

- Teaches that war is an acceptable way of settling disputes
- Encourages pretending to kill or hurt others
- Falsely glamorizes military life, combat and war
- Depicts ethnic or racial groups in a negative way
- Fosters unnecessary, aggressive competition
- Teaches violence to the earth
- Creates the need for an enemy

Some people say that playing with toy guns is not dangerous and teaches children the importance of knowing how to protect themselves. Read the following newspaper article and think about this teenager and thousands of others every day who get hurt or killed because of "pretend" war.

> **Deputy Slays Teenager
> Wielding Toy Laser Gun**
>
> A San Bernardino County Sheriff's deputy, summoned to investigate a late night report of armed prowlers at a school yard, shot and killed a teenager who, along with three companions, had been playing a popular make-believe game with toy laser guns, authorities said Wednesday. A department spokesman said this boy "jumped out from the dark and posed in a shooting stance, pointing a gun at the deputy. The deputy never had time to identify himself as a law enforcement officer."

G. I. Joe Has Got to Go

Aggressive play leads to acts of real aggression; it invites you to think of others as enemies and objects and, therefore, makes you less sensitive to human beings. Think of the last time you played an aggressive game or played with war toys.

1. Did you have to create an "enemy"?

2. Who was the enemy?

3. When you had an "enemy," what kind of thoughts did you have about this enemy?

4. What did you feel toward this enemy?

HERE LIES
John J. Smith
DIED IN ACTION 1971
GAVE HIS LIFE FOR
HIS COUNTRY
AND FOR FREEDOM

DIED IN ACTION

5. Did you think of this enemy as a person, with a name, an address, a personality, a family?

Aggressive play may temporarily help you get rid of pent-up resentment and hostile feelings, but there are other, more beneficial ways to help you do this. If you feel hostile, there is a good reason for it. You need to talk out those feelings—not play war.

✈ Television commercials often put great pressure on you to buy war games, toys and videos.

✈ Toys usually teach more than we are aware of. Dolls help you learn to be a parent, and tanks and guns teach you to make war.

✈ TV cartoons can teach that anyone who disagrees with you is an "enemy."

✈ From war games, you learn that deception and lying are good ways to deal with problems, that killing is a way to show your superiority, and that uniforms give you strength.

What Are We Learning from G. I. Joe?

Did you know that sales of G. I. Joe war toys total over $100 million a year? Violent role models like Rambo and He-Man are found in movies, books, on TV, comics and videos, on lunch boxes, book bags, clothing, sheets, blankets, curtains. There is even G. I. Joe cereal and Rambo gum. Saturday morning cartoons show these violent characters on TV. The G.I. Joe cartoon show features eighty-four acts of violence per hour—that's more than one act of violence *every minute*. You and your brothers and sisters have watched them or are watching them regularly.

**Did you know that
80,000 Barbie dolls have been sold
in military outfits since the Gulf War?**

Video Games

There are lots of video games in the marketplace that bring out the warrior in you. You might think war-based video games are just harmless fun, but the military takes them very seriously; did you know that the U.S. Army has used Nintendo games to train soldiers for fighting real wars? As long as you are aware of the impact of these games, you may be less likely to be pulled into a warrior state of mind.

1.   What is a common story line in video games?

2.   What is the object of military video games?

3.   Do video games cause you to think in terms of the most effective use of force and power to kill?

4. What is the usual role of a female in these games?

5. Are "power" and "victory" the main point of these games?

6. Is there any attempt in these games to "talk things out" or to think of helping one's opponent?

7. Is victory the only goal?

8. Are there nonviolent video games as well as violent ones? Which ones are they?

9. What are your favorite computer games?

10. What's your definition of a terrific computer game?

✍ ✍ ✍

Activity: Create a Peaceful Video Game!

This activity can be done alone or with one or more friends. If there are more than six of you, break into two teams. Imagine that you work for a video manufacturer or a toy company and it's your job to create a peaceful video game— a game with no violence.

✓   What will your storyline be? Where will this video game take place? How many characters will you use?

✓   How can you make the video game fun without being violent or having your characters do violent things?

✓   Give the female in your storyline the part that you would traditionally give to the male. Giva a male in your storyline a part that you would typically give to a female.

✓   Will there be young people in this game? What roles will they play?

✓   What will be your main source of conflict, and how will you go about resolving it?

✓   What will be the goal of this game?

✓   How will characters work out problems between them?

137

✓   What will you call your video game?

If you have broken into teams, read your video game descriptions to each other and compare them for excitement and fun. Please note: If you want to send your ideas to us, please do so; we're always interested in what young people think about war and peace. Our address is at the back of this book.

✍ ✍ ✍

HOW CAN I AVOID BECOMING
A WARRIOR?

Chapter 12

PEACE IS POSSIBLE!

Toys and Activities That Celebrate Life

When countries go through times of war, toy companies look for ways to make a profit. They do so by manufacturing war toys.

There are hundreds of other toys and activities that are fun, exciting and that celebrate life. If you are about to celebrate a birthday or other holiday or go to someone else's birthday for which you are going to purchase a present, encourage relatives and friends not to give warlike gifts, but to give, and help you give, one of the following instead:

☞   A visit to a museum, nature shop, aquarium
☞   Books, cassettes, marbles, world globe
☞   Model cars, planes, glider, ecology game
☞   Astronomy map, microscope set, potter's wheel
☞   Art supplies, stickers, paint easels, arts and crafts
☞   Puzzles, kites, soccer ball, posters, jewelry box
☞   Music boxes, sports equipment, roller skates
☞   Velcro dart board, gardening tools, chemistry set
☞   Clay, wood and carving tools, dance lessons
☞   Martial arts lessons (the right kind), sleeping bag
☞   Cameras, games, binoculars, singing lessons

☞　　Dance or concert tickets, surf board, fun clothes
☞　　Bicycles and skates, leotards, running clothes
☞　　Camping trip, backpack, hiking boots, equipment

Perhaps we can help toy manufacturers come up with more exciting toys and games that promote a peaceful life rather than a warlike life. Here's an activity that will inspire you to create one of them.

✍　　✍　　✍

Activity: Create a Game or Toy for Peace

✓　Think of your favorite game. If it's a game that encourages competition and warlike behavior, think of a way to change the game into a peaceful one.

✓　If your favorite game is a peaceful game, think of another game, a new game, based on it. Are there characters you would add to the game? Are there special rules that would help resolve problems or situations nonviolently?

✓　What's your favorite toy? Create a peaceful game you could play with that toy. Would you need other toys?

✓　What would you call your game? How many can play?

✓　What would be the peaceful objective of your exciting game?

142

Take a look at the difference between celebrating life and playing war. I think you probably already know what they are:

Playing War Teaches Us to:	**Celebrating Life Teaches Us to:**
Make two sides: ours and theirs	Get along together
Solve arguments by fighting	Solve arguments by talking
Learn about guns & war tactics	Learn everyday skills
Reward violence and aggression	Reward co-existence in harmony
Start fights and make enemies	Start projects and make friends
Pretend people don't suffer and die	Help people thrive and survive
Make enemies of people not like us	Value people of all backgrounds
Make boys seem more important	Respect all girls and boys

For a list of more positive toys and games, you can write to the following organizations:

The Campaign for Progressive Toys and Games
Cumberland Center for Justice & Peace
P. O. Box 857
Sewanee, TN 37375

National Association for the Education of Young Children
1834 Connecticut Avenue, N.W.
Washington, DC 20009
(800) 424-2460 or (202) 232-8777

Children's Creative Response to Conflict
P.O. Box 271, 523 North Broadway
Nyack, NY 10960
(914) 358-4601

Children and Nonviolence Campaign
c/o War Resisters League
339 Lafayette Street
New York, NY 10012
(212) 228-0450

Questions:

1. Do you think playing with war toys can lead to wanting to use the real thing as an adult? Why?

2. If you are denied guns and war toys, does this make you want them more? If you are told not to touch a hot stove burner, does this make you want to touch it more? What's the difference?

3. Do you think war toys help you get rid of violent feelings, or do you think they create or increase violent feelings?

4. Can talking over aggressive feelings with trusted friends, parents or teachers help release them in healthy ways? If so, why?

5. Do you think children's toy advertisers are more

concerned with making great toys or making great profits?

6. Do you think you could be just as happy without play guns and war toys of any kind? If not, why?

7. Do you think a uniform gives you strength? If not, what do you think really gives you strength?

8. What excites a young person about playing with war toys?

9. What other exciting nonviolent activities can take the place of playing at war?

10. In what ways does "playing guns" differ from actual war?

Chapter 13

TEACHING PEACE

Can you guess what this ad is for?

Help Wanted
Deck hands. Immediate opening with international maritime organization seeking to man rapidly expanding fleet. Relocation necessary at our expense. On the job training, good salary, excellent benefits, world travel. Ages 17-34. High school diploma required. Must be in good physical condition.

The above is an actual ad that appeared in a newspaper. Can you see how it was designed to deliberately hide its military origins?

You learned in a previous chapter that the military is more than a couple of years of service, that it is, in fact, a way of life. Over the years, the military has created places that teach war—military academies. For thousands of years humans have trained in these academies to learn how to defend themselves from other humans by killing. In order to have peace we need to open institutions that teach peace and instruct us how to resolve conflict *non*violently.

✎   ✎   ✎

Activity: Create a Peace Academy

✓   If you were to start a new school, one that taught all we need to know about living a peaceful life—individually and globally—how would you begin?

✓   Would you study Military Academies to find out what they do, and then do the opposite?

✓   Would you help people learn to solve conflicts by talking with one another rather than fighting or killing one another?

✓   Make a list of the subjects you would teach.

✓   Make a list of the actions you would reward with a medal.

✓   How would you define a peace hero?

✎   ✎   ✎

Once you have created your own lists, take a look at the lists I have compiled on the next page, and compare them.

MILITARY ACADEMY ⇒	**PEACE ACADEMY**
Teaches: ⇒	**Teaches:**
The history of war	The history of peace
Military scientific research	Environmental research
Defense research	Conflict resolution
Controlling others through fear	Order through understanding
How to kill	How to respect
Gives medals for: ⇒	**Gives medals for:**
Killing others	Nonviolent conflict resolution
Being wounded	Healing old wounds
The military hero: ⇒	**The peace hero:**
Conforms to a common goal	Balances goals
Accepts without questions	Looks at facts with no bias
Is able-bodied	Has an able body *and* mind
Values group thinking	Values individual thinking
Destroys enemy forces	Understands different thinking
Learns to obey any command	Questions when in doubt
Learns by rote	Debates, thinks creatively
Exploits enemy weakness	Looks for mutual strengths
Deceives to attain power	Sees truth is power
Is a male	Is either male or female
Offers military solutions to world problems	Offers peaceful solutions to world problems

✌ ✌ ✌

Questions:

1. Can Military Academies create peaceful people?

2. Do you think teaching people how to kill will create a peaceful world?

3. Why do you think we don't have Peace Academies?

4. Do you think Peace Academies would do well? Why or why not?

5. Who would be your ideal staff for a Peace Academy? What qualifications should your staff have?

6. Are there advantages in looking at the world with the eyes of the Peace Hero? What are they?

7. Do you think it's a good thing to look at facts without any bias or judgment?

8. Are most people accustomed to judging everything they see?

9. Do you think judgment creates conflict? If so, how?

10. Is understanding conflict important to you?

Chapter 14

WAR—WHAT IS IT GOOD FOR?

We outlaw stealing and murder but we give people medals and honor them in glorious parades when they've gone to war and killed each other. Does this make sense? Isn't war just mass murder? How do we justify doing this while saying we care about people?

Can We Outlaw War?

Do you know of any organization or country that has actually outlawed war? There are many laws protecting people from other people who would do them harm. But I know of no law that outlaws war—the greatest crime ever that humans do against their own kind. There have been thousands of treaties and temporary laws banning certain weapons or certain countries' military activities, but as far as I know, there is no generally agreed upon law that makes war a crime.

The United Nations is supposed to be an organization that helps create peace and goodwill among the peoples of the earth. What we have neglected to realize is that we cannot unite nations together into one big whole. "United" means whole; "nations" means separate groups. If the leaders of the

world could see the problem at the root of the "United Nations," each would end his or her "membership," or allegiance to his or her particular group. The "global members" would then vote to outlaw war forever as a way to resolve human problems. Has the United Nations outlawed war? If not, why? They have a "Peacekeeping" army, but it's well-armed and looks just like any other army. *War cannot bring about peace!* In order to outlaw war, we would not let *anyone* commit it. Leaders of countries who encourage war would be brought to justice and prevented from warring.

Can We Ban Military Arms?

The greatest single thing we can do to outlaw war, to *prevent* it, is *to stop making armaments*! People who make, sell, or trade military arms, in my view, are commiting a crime. Some of those people say that they need the job, that they are only making a living. Some justify it by saying that the "enemy" makes them, so "we" must make them. These excuses are not sane arguments. There are other jobs. There are *non*violent alternatives to resolve conflict. Once weapons are produced and put into the hands of warriors, it's just a matter of time before they are used in combat. You may have heard that the threat of war is the best way to insure peace—that "a strong offense is the best defense"—but it's just not true. If we keep on justifying the making of death machines, then we will keep on making war—and it will never end—except perhaps if we are all killed!

Can we:

- Form an "Outlaw War" group?
- Get petitions signed outlawing war?
- Send letters and petitions to national leaders?
- Talk to younger kids about playing at war?
- Talk to friends who may be thinking of joining the military?
- Take a field trip to the United Nations (in New York City, U.S.A., or one of its global offices) and meet with international leaders to get their support for outlawing war?

If you want to live a peaceful life, if you love your friends, parents and relatives, you will need to find ways to promote outlawing war. And by now you know you *can* do it!

Remember—war is hazardous to our health!

Questions:

1. Is it possible to outlaw war?

2. Do you feel war should be outlawed?

3. Who should outlaw war?

4.   What part can you play in outlawing war?

5.   What would be your first step in outlawing war?

6.   Can peace be kept by military force?

7.   Can war bring peace—ever?

8.   What do you think about companies that manufac-
     ture arms?

9.   Do you think the government should find new jobs
     for people who make their living selling weapons?

10. If war is hazardous to our health, why do we go to
     war?

Chapter 15

MARTIAL ARTS FOR PEACE

Something in Common—A Story

Leon walked quietly down the school corridor. It was after school and he was one of the last students around. He turned the corner and there they were—Vinnie and his two buddies, the school bullies.

"Remember Leon, when you see them again, don't let your fear get the better of you. We've practiced for the occasion many times," he heard his Martial Arts instructor saying in his mind.

Vinnie and his two buddies stood in front of the exit to the school. Leon could have turned around and walked the other way, but he wasn't going to run this time. Running away hurt him emotionally and made him feel like a wimp. Every time he ran away, he felt unsettled, unresolved. Leon recalled the sound of Vinnie's voice yelling at him, "Coward, come back and I'll show you who's boss!"

"OK, guys, here I am. I guess you're going to beat me up. It's no use hiding anymore," Leon said as he approached the three boys.

On seeing Leon coming forward with confidence, Vinnie and his buddies felt slightly uneasy. This was not their victim's usual style.

"Hey, man. Let's go a round or two!" Vinnie squinted his

dark eyes and tried to look tough.

"Well, if you insist. We can go outside if you want. Or we can go down to the Karate school and go a few rounds." Leon spoke confidently, looking Vinnie straight in the eye. Leon positioned himself with the wall behind him so he couldn't be attacked from the back.

"Yeah, you think you're so tough now with that martial arts stuff. Come on, Kung-fu fool, show me your moves," one of Vinnie's buddies called out from behind Vinnie.

"Yeah, come on," Vinnie repeated. "What would you do if I came at you like this," Vinnie jumped forward with a few fake punches which Leon dodged easily.

"Fast on your feet! Try this one," Vinnie shouted, trying to kick Leon. Leon again evaded the kick, easily moving from side to side with a professional karate stance.

"Look, Vinnie, someone is going to get hurt. I really don't want to fight. How about us calling a truce?" Leon said gently.

"Truce? Hey, man, I'm not your friend! I'm here to bother you."

"In that case, I guess we'll just have to fight. But before we do, do you mind if just you and I go at it? I mean you're stronger and tougher than your buddies. You can take me on alone," Leon responded with a smile.

"Whadda' ya' think, I'm going to mess my hair just for you? Go on, get lost. I don't need it." Vinnie spoke with a false confidence.

"Well, thanks for letting me off," Leon said, easing the tension. "I don't think I could have won anyway. My Karate teacher told me never to fight."

"So long, man. Until next time. See you around," Vinnie

said sarcastically. Vinnie and his two buddies turned away from Leon and walked out the front door into the afternoon sun.

"Good, Leon," his teacher told him later that day at practice. "You had the confidence not to fight, to win by losing. It was good that we practiced nonviolent alternatives. Do you think they worked?"

"Yes," Leon smiled. "I felt a whole lot more confident this time knowing both sets of skills—my martial arts self-defense skills and my martial arts nonviolent alternatives—knowing that if they came at me, I had a good chance of not getting beaten up. And knowing how to use my brain to get out of trouble really gave me double confidence. Those nonviolent alternatives really work when I practice them."

The next day Leon was at school when he saw Vinnie standing near the cafeteria. Vinnie was alone. He didn't see Leon behind him. Leon stopped quietly and really looked at Vinnie, without seeing him as a bully, without, for a moment, knowing who he was. He saw a hard, sad young person. Vinnie was not aware of himself at that moment as he stood there looking out the window. Leon suddenly felt sorry for his former enemy. He could see through that toughness to see a young man who himself had been bullied. Leon could tell that all the anger stored inside of Vinnie had come from a great hurt inside him. For a moment that hurt showed itself for Leon to see.

"Nice day," Leon said, announcing himself. Vinnie suddenly stiffened and his body went hard. He turned around with steely eyes and met Leon's.

"I'm not your enemy," Leon suddenly said without knowing why. "I actually want to be your friend, if you can believe it."

Vinnie's face softened and a small smile slowly shone through the tough surface.

"Yeah, ya' think so, man? You and me, friends? What for?" he asked cautiously, with a tough attitude.

"I don't know. I just think we've got something in common, that's all."

"What, you and me, alike? That's a laugh."

"Well, perhaps we're into the same thing," Leon spoke again.

"What?"

"Motorcycles! That's what," Leon said with a laugh. "I heard you talking about 'em in the cafeteria yesterday. My Mom's ready to ground me for hanging around so much at the cycle shop downtown."

"Oh, man, you got that right! I love a fast bike," Vinnie laughed out loud. Leon had never really seen him laugh before.

Vinnie jokingly punched Leon in the arm as they walked down the hall.

"Bikes, yeah bikes," Vinnie said. "Yeah, we got something in common," he laughed.

War Is a Playground

Later that day Leon sat thinking of Vinnie and the sadness he saw in him. Leon's teacher was talking about war and peace. It was his sixth-period Social Science class.

"What do you think creates war?" his teacher spoke, bringing Leon back from his daydream.

"People are hurt," he said suddenly. "They are hurt and want to protect themselves. They are afraid of being hurt again so they get defensive and tough and act like bullies."

"Where did you learn that?" his teacher asked, responding to Leon's statement. The whole class had turned around to look at Leon.

"Well, I first thought about it in my Martial Arts class. We talk about conflict and war there. My Martial Arts teacher says that the Martial Arts help you understand conflict, to be peaceful. They do, too. I think nations are just people, like you and me. I mean, we create wars. I remember fighting in the playground when I was younger. I think war is like that. It's like a big playground with bullies and guys that get picked on."

"That's great, Leon!" his teacher went on. "Maybe understanding war is not so difficult, when you look at the basic causes. After all, as you said, we are all just people; we are afraid, we get hurt, and we want to hurt back. And it's interesting that you learned about it in a Martial Arts class. I thought Martial Arts was violent. If you look at those Martial Arts films, it sure seems like it!"

"Well, that's true, but those movies are made in Hollywood. They don't give the right idea of what the Martial Arts really are—at least the way my teacher teaches them. He says the Martial Arts are a great way to understand yourself, to look at why you are afraid and how you create conflict, even war. It's really interesting," Leon answered his teacher.

"It sounds like everyone should study the Martial Arts with a teacher like that. Tell us more as you learn about conflict and war."

163

Leaving school that day, Leon felt more grown up. He understood now what his Martial Arts teacher was telling him and he began to feel that his classes were very important. "Remember, Leon, to end conflict without fighting is the highest skill," his teacher said to him. Leon thought that perhaps someday he too might be a Martial Arts teacher.

> **If you have understood by now that war begins in you, with the way you've been conditioned to think and act, you will see that war can also end in you.**

Let's look at the nonviolent alternatives that Leon was talking about and find out how we can use them.

Do I Fight or Do I Run?

If you were confronted by a bully, what would you do? Freeze? Fight? Run away?

Have you ever noticed a cat and dog when they suddenly meet? What happens? Does the cat fight or run away? All it knows is to fight or to run. Its instinct to survive tells it that it must do one of these things.

Did you know that humans have this survival reaction too? It's built into the brain. Psychologists, people who are trained to deal with mental and emotional problems, call this the "Fight or Flight Response." It is an automatic response that helps us cope with danger and meet our need to survive.

For example, if you are crossing the street and a car out of control races toward you, your "fight or flight response" lights up "Flight!" in your brain and tells you to run, fast. Our biological instinct for self-preservation, for survival, responds to this physical threat. This response has been part of us since humans were cave creatures who had to fight or run away from a dangerous animal. Today, when you meet up with a bully, this fight or flight reaction still happens. In your mind you see either "Fight!" or "Flight!"

When confronted—not by a car out of control, but by another human being by whom we feel threatened—our brain responds in the same way, automatically. We feel threatened and afraid, and our brain tells us to either fight or run away. Our brain has been conditioned to think: This person is an enemy, someone I must fight, someone I must go to war with. We react as if the threat is physical, but sometimes it's not. It's almost always just a psychological threat—one that happens in our minds.

There is a better, safer way to deal with psychological threats.
Becoming a warrior and fighting others
can never bring about peace.
Violence can bring only one thing:
more violence.

Learning how to fight for peace is learning nonviolent alternatives to fighting. Have you seen or studied the Martial Arts? Many of you have seen the Martial Arts in television and movies depicted as violent. This is *not* what the Martial Arts

166

should be. The proper practice of Martial Arts includes the study of *two* skills: physical self-defense moves AND nonviolent mental techniques. There are Martial Arts schools that teach only self-defense moves. This makes for an unbalanced martial artist. It is equally as important to learn nonviolent psychological techniques.

The most powerful tool you have is something you carry around with you all the time: your mind.

Movie makers do not show you these psychological skills, because they believe that fighting and killing arc more exciting. Those of us who have practiced nonviolent alternatives and seen them work find them extremely exciting because they have helped resolve conflicts *without* fighting and have eliminated the only real enemy we have: fear.

If you learn self-defense skills only, you will have the confidence to handle many situations with a bully, at least physically. But this may be dangerous because you have only one option—fighting. If you learn nonviolent alternatives to fighting along with self-defense skills, you will have confidence AND will know how to solve many conflicts WITHOUT fighting. Here are some alternatives you could use in getting out of a fight without fighting. Think them through, practice them over and over. Perhaps your parents, teachers or friends can help. In the section that follows, you will read about ways to practice these nonviolent alternatives.

NONVIOLENT ALTERNATIVES

Make Friends Treat the bully as a friend; lots of bullies don't have many friends. ("You and I have something in common. We both like motorcycles.")

Use Humor Sometimes you can stop a fight by being funny or telling a joke. But be careful! Make fun of the situation, not the bully.

Walk Away Refuse to comply with the bully's wishes. Turn around and walk away confidently.

Agree If the bully says you are a wimp, agree with the bully. Don't let the bully's words (or your "agreement") get you angry. ("You're right. I'm weak, and everyone knows it. So what's left to prove? See you in class. Goodbye.")

Refuse to Fight No matter what, don't fight! ("Hit me if you want to, but I'm not going to fight. I don't believe in fighting. I believe in talking. Want to talk about something? What's the problem?")

Stand up to the Bully Standing up to a bully means that you tell him or her with words, with your body, with how you present yourself, that you won't be bullied.

Trickery	Pretend you are sick or that you are about to meet someone. ("My friend, Bob, who's a boxer, is taking me to the doctor—I've got poison ivy, which is catchy, by the way.") Trickery is not lying; it is just using your creative imagination to get out of conflict nonviolently.
Ignore the Bully	This is an alternative that requires caution. When you ignore the bully, you pretend he or she is not there. You may want to use this in combination with walking away or trickery.
Use Authority	Show the bully you are not afraid and will not allow him or her to hurt you. You can call someone else to help you who is more powerful than the bully—someone who is older or in power, like a parent, teacher or police officer. Or be your own authority; use your own power.
Use Reason or Talk It Out	Learning to reason or talk it out requires practice. Think out what you want to say and rehearse your approach over and over. Here, as in all nonviolent alternatives, you are exercising the strongest muscle you have—that muscle between your ears!

Questions:

1. In the story, how was Leon's approach to the bullies different after talking to the Martial Arts instructor?

2.   When the bullies decided not to fight with Leon, how did Leon respond? Did he antagonize them, or did he back off?

3.   Do you think Leon's new self-confidence helped him back off without feeling like a coward?

4.   What skill combination made Leon feel more confident?

5.   Can you see how both physical defense skills and psychological nonviolent alternatives give you more confidence together? How?

6.   Do you agree with Leon that nations are just people, like you and me? If yes, why?

7.   Do you think that when we get scared and hurt, we immediately want to fight or run away? Why?

8.   What nonviolent alternatives to fighting can you use when you feel threatened or frightened?

9.   Do you think you can help put an end to war?

10. What would be your first step in attempting to put an end to war?

Stopping Conflict Before It Starts—a Role-play

Here is an example of how to practice what you have just learned—the nonviolent alternatives:

When you are learning to play basketball or learning how to play a musical instrument, the way you get better is to practice. The same goes for using nonviolent alternatives. The way we practice them is to participate in an exercise called "role-play." Have you ever heard of role-playing? It's like acting in a play.

Here is an example of such a play, with two characters. Perhaps you can find a friend or family member to play this out with. Dale is the tough bully, and Jan, a new person in town, is a gentle person—strong, but very calm.

Dale: (Angry) "You're the new kid, isn't that right?"

Jan: (Calm) "That's right. My name is Jan."

Dale: "What makes you think I have the slightest interest in knowing your name?"

Jan: "It's a courtesy to tell people your name when you first meet."

Dale: "Well, I don't believe in courtesy. And I don't want to know the name of any new-kid foreigner."

Jan: "I hope I'm not a foreigner for long."

Dale: "We don't like foreigners much here. You should take my advice and get out of here— soon."

Jan: "I like it here. *Some* people I've met are very friendly."

Dale: "Well, you don't look like you belong here, kid."

Jan: "Sorry about that. I didn't think people had to look a certain way in order to belong. I thought people were people. (Pause.) Isn't your name Dale?"

Dale: "Never mind my name. If you want to belong here, you better be ready to fight to prove it."

Jan: "Look, I don't want to fight. I'm not a fighter. Besides, you're bigger than I am. Can't we be friends?

Dale: "You foreigners think you can come here and take over our town. You think you can rob us, like one foreigner did last year!"

Jan: "I don't want to rob you. Come on, let's shake hands."

Dale: (Slaps Jan's hand away.) "I don't shake with foreigners." (Walks away.)

Questions:

1. Have you met people like Dale?

2. If you were Jan, would you be afraid of Dale?

3. Was there a point where you felt Jan ought to fight or run away?

4. Which of these characters do you relate to the most?

5. Have you experienced a conversation like this one?

6. Have you bullied someone? What happened?

7. Have you been bullied by someone? What happened?

8. Do you think Dale was afraid?

9. What was Dale afraid of?

10. Do you think there's hope for Dale and Jan being friends?

✍   ✍   ✍

Activity: Creating a Role-play

✓   Create a role-play by writing down on paper certain dialogue lines that characters will say. If you need help, ask the assistance of a trusted adult, a teacher or community leader.

✓   Create a "bully" scene in which a bully finds it hard to be friendly toward someone else.

✓   Create a "victim" scene in which a victim thinks up ways to resolve conflict nonviolently, using any or all of the nonviolent alternatives discussed before—yours and mine.

✓   Have fun working out how to get out of the bully situation without fighting. Be as creative as you like! Enjoy the challenge!

✓   Get some help to "act out" the role-play. Get into your part and have fun with it!

✓   What did you learn by writing this role-play? What did you learn by acting it out?

✓   Do you think working on role-plays can help you work out real problems that you have?

✍   ✍   ✍

Fighting for Peace

When you fight for peace:

❶ You can learn physical self-defense skills —not to hurt someone, but to protect yourself and gain confidence in potentially hostile situations.

❷ You can learn psychological (mental) self-defense skills through role-playing, using the nonviolent alternatives we just went over.

❸ You purposely engage in *not* fighting.

A new way of thinking:

You learn how to fight,
which gives you the confidence
to do everything in your power *not* to fight.

Does it sound too easy? Well, it takes lots of practice, physically and mentally, but it can work! If you are skilled in using nonviolent alternatives, you will learn to end conflict *before* it starts.

A Special Note to Those Interested
in Studying the Martial Arts

You may think it doesn't make sense to study the martial arts in order to have peace. But it really helps, *if* it is taught in the right way. I've practiced and taught the Martial Arts for over thirty years. Their main intent is truly to learn how to resolve conflict peacefully. To learn this all-encompassing art, one must practice BOTH physical self-defense skills and psychological (mental) self-defense skills (non-violent alternatives).

Practice physical moves with your body.
Practice nonviolent alternatives with your mind.

The two go together. Learning both sets of skills leads to resolving conflict with your brain rather than your brawn.

If it is your intention to study the Martial Arts, seek out a school with a teacher who will show you both sets of skills.

Questions:

1.   When you create a role-play between a bully and a victim, does it help you understand the minds of both the bully and the victim?

2.   Can you see how both physical defense skills and

176

psychological nonviolent alternatives give you more confidence together?

3.   Why do you think so much stress is put on NOT fighting?

4.   Can you imagine being able to stop conflict *before* it starts?

5.   How do you think this could help you in your life now? As an adult?

6.   What are some specific ways solving conflict as a young person will help you grow into a more intelligent adult?

7.   If we can learn how to resolve individual conflict before it starts, what effect will this have on the extreme social conflict, war?

8.   Does it make sense to you that the Martial Arts, if studied in peaceful ways, can bring about peace — both individually and globally? Why?

9.   How does learning how to fight create peace?

10. Do you think that the Martial Arts, as described in this chapter, should be taught in school as a regular part of the curriculum? Why?

Chapter 16

WHAT CAN I DO?

Do you sometimes feel helpless in a huge world with so much conflict? There are times when I do, but you and I *can* do something—many things—to bring about peace. As a matter of fact, you already know a great deal more than you did before. You know:

❶ There are two specific root causes of war:

○ Identification (with a group or tribe)

○ Projection (that "other" party is my "enemy")

❷ We have seen how the brain causes conflict by creating an "enemy." As soon as we create an enemy (and all enemies are created in our minds), we have a need for a hero warrior to save us from this enemy.

❸ We have created Warhawk, a robot hero, fed it with automatic conditioned responses, and trained it to be a warrior. By becoming aware of this training and conditioning, we are more aware of people who might try to condition us to want to become warriors, to join military organizations, to learn to be hostile, fighting creatures.

❹   We have looked at how girls and boys can become warriors. We have seen how, in today's world, we have learned to be aggressive and competitive, believing this is necessary for our survival.

❺   We have seen how being "patriotic"—unquestioningly supportive of a country—can be dangerous to ourselves and the world as a whole, because this kind of patriotism makes an instant "enemy" out of anyone who does not feel patriotic to "our" country.

❻   We have looked at the Martial Arts and learned what it considers the greatest achievement—to end conflict *without* fighting.

We have come a long way, but there is more we can do. If you have decided you do not want to become a warrior, that there are more intelligent and peaceful ways to resolve the problems of human relationship than by going to war—then this section is for you, because here you will learn about what you and your friends, parents, teachers and community leaders can do to help make sure that peace is the way we solve our conflicts from now on.

> **Start by saying to yourself:**
> **PEACE BEGINS WITH ME.**

The Enlightened Veteran

Some people go to war, return, and celebrate their service. Others return feeling misled and make the decision to speak their minds about their experiences to young people like you. These returnees go into the Armed Forces believing in their country, their political system, and their leaders. They trusted that their way of life is superior to all others, and that any nation or people who oppose them must be bad or wrong. Many of these returnees feel, after their services, that they themselves were the aggressors, the ones who were destroying forests with chemicals and burning fields with napalm (a fire-bomb).

The Conscientious Objector—Preparing for the Draft

Accurate knowledge is available to you if you have the courage and tenacity to seek it out.

Citizens who claim conscientious objector status are viewed dimly by the military. Yet there are many men and women who find war in general, or a single war in particular, so repugnant that participation would offend their moral understanding. Many responded in this way to the Gulf War and to every other war that has preceded it.

Although at the time this book was written no United States military draft was in effect, the military can, in the event of war, draft young people to fight whether they want to or not. The draft law provides exemption for people who cannot take part in war because they think it would be wrong to do so. To be a conscientious objector (CO), you must object to all wars, but you need not object to all use of force, nor must you know what you would do in every situation. You can object on religious or moral grounds, or both. To be officially classified a conscientious objector takes some time and effort, but it is one of the only legal ways to avoid being made to fight in a war.

Depending on what your conscience would permit, you would be classified either 1-0 or 1-A-0. 1-0 objectors do civilian work under civilian direction. 1-A-0 objectors become noncombatant (unarmed) soldiers.

You can register with the Central Committee For Conscientious Objectors (CCCO) using their "Conscientious Objector Card." This will provide a record of your position on war and may help a later claim which you make to your draft board. The CCCO was founded in 1948 to aid conscientious objectors not covered by the law. It also provides legal support for draft resisters and counsels COs seeking discharge from the military, as well as young men and women considering whether to enlist in the military.

Few people know how conscientious objectors are sometimes treated. The Military Conscientious Objector Act of 1992 allows personnel to object to specific wars. The War Resisters League says more than 2,500 people applied for discharge as conscientious objectors (COs) during the Gulf War. Many applications were "lost" or rejected outright, and many applicants were abused by their superior officers. Several were jailed in military bases, and some are still awaiting trial for "violating the military code."

Some reservist COs stand to lose their civilian jobs. Some have been convicted of "missing a movement" after filing for CO status and medical discharge claims, which the armed services

OUTLAW WAR
HONOR VETERANS NO MORE WAR
4310
NATIONAL RECRUITING OFFICE
ARMY
NAVY
AIR FORCE
MARINES

IN THE ARMY... BE ALL THAT YOU CAN BE!
YOUTH FOR PEACE AND JUSTICE
STOP THE ARMS RACE NOT THE HUMAN RACE!
PRACTICE NON-VIOLENCE
ONE EARTH ONE PEOPLE

refused to process. Some are still locked in military prisons for desertion; some stand to lose their professional status by having medical or teaching licenses revoked.

An outpouring of letters from hundreds of thousands of people have freed some of these COs and have caused congressional investigation into the way the armed forces conducts military justice. Legislation that assures fair treatment to CO applicants has been introduced into Congress.

What You Can Do to Become a Conscientious Objector

Have you thought about what you would do if you were required to go to war? Have you considered finding alternatives to the military if the draft were reinstated? In order to understand what your alternatives are, talk to someone you trust; discuss your questions and contact someone at one of the addresses below (for information on CO status in the United States):

Central Committee for Conscientious Objectors (CCCO)
2208 South Street
Philadelphia, PA 19146
(215) 545-4626

Central Committee for Conscientious Objectors (CCCO)
P. O. Box 42249
San Francisco, CA 94142
(415) 474-3002

Militarism Resource Project
P. O. Box 13416
Philadelphia, PA 19101-3416

National Campaign to Demilitarize Our Schools
(NCDOS)
1501 Cherry Street
Philadelphia, PA 19102

Veterans Education Project
P. O. Box 416
Amherst, MA 01004-0416
(413) 549-5037
(A non-profit organization of speakers)

Citizen Soldier
175 Fifth Avenue, Suite 808
New York, NY 10010
(212) 777-3470

Fellowship of Reconciliation (FOR)
P.O. Box 271
Nyack, NY 10960
(914) 358-4601

There Are Other Choices

It is hard to find a job today, but it can be done. Before
you make the decision to join the military because you feel it's
the only place left to find work, talk to your friends and neigh-

bors who are employed and ask how they got their jobs. Talk to guidance counselors and teachers. They have resources and connections you may be able to use to find a job—and they may also be able to help if you are interested in vocational training or community college. Other organizations that could help include neighborhood job counseling programs, youth employment groups, city and state employment agencies and union training programs.

One peaceful alternative to joining the military is becoming an apprentice to a skilled worker in a trade that interests you. There are more than a hundred jobs—from Air Conditioner Mechanic to Welder—which offer apprenticeship programs. You can learn more about the programs, how to qualify and how to apply for them, by writing to:

Bureau of Apprenticeship and Training
U.S. Department of Labor
601 D Street, NW
Room 6100
Washington DC 20213

Labor unions offer training programs to help people enter such fields as carpentry, steel working, printing, etc. To get information on union training and apprenticeships, write:

Department of Education, AFL-CIO
101 Constitution Avenue, NW
Washington, DC 20001

If you are an American who is strongly interested in helping people in developing countries in Africa, Asia, or elsewhere, you would be a good candidate for the Peace Corps. Most Peace Corps volunteers are at least 21 years old, but younger men and women are chosen too—especially if they have farming, construction or similar "hands-on" experience.

Peace Corps
1990 K Street N.W.
Washington, D. C.
(202) 638-2574 or (800) 424-8580

There are many books to help you as you search for a job and a career. Because so much money is spent to recruit and train soldiers, most employment guides for young people include information on how to become a member of the Armed Services. Some of the books listed below do. But if you are aware of what it really means to become a warrior, and want to discover *nonviolent* alternatives to a military career, you will find plenty of helpful material in these books:

CAREER FINDER:
Pathways to Over 1500 Entry-Level Jobs.
Lester Schwartz and Irv Brechner.
Ballantine, 1990.

COLLEGE BOARD GUIDE TO JOBS AND CAREER PLANNING.
Joyce Slayton Mitchell.
The College Board, 1992.

GUIDE TO APPRENTICESHIP PROGRAMS.
William F. Shanahan.
Arco Occupational Guides, 1983.

YOU CAN MAKE IT WITHOUT A COLLEGE DEGREE.
Roberta Roesch.
Simon & Schuster, 1986.

What You Can Do To Help

Becoming a conscientious objector to war, and seeking a nonmilitary job are just a couple of things you can do to oppose war. Here are several examples of other actions you could take that would promote peace in your life, among your classmates, and across the globe:

○ Contact your congressional representatives to let them know your views on recruiter access to schools.

○ Press your school board to pass a resolution prohibiting the release of student information to military recruiters or, at a minimum, ensuring that peace activists are guaranteed "equal time" when recruiters are present.

○ Speak to PTA and community groups about the impact of military recruiting in the schools.

○ Discuss the values taught by the military: conformity, unquestioned obedience to authority, and a lack of individual responsibility.

○   Seek to get a peace presentation in the schools. There are probably many professional peace activists in your area willing to speak to students. Or ask a combat veteran to share his experiences in the military.

○   Research and produce an "alternatives directory" of non-military job and educational opportunities in your community. Your directory could be distributed to other interested students by your school's guidance office.

The Peace Movement

Have you ever heard of the peace movement? While people have tried to solve the problems of relationship with violence and war, there have been millions of people who have tried to resolve conflict peacefully. There are thousands of organizations worldwide that work full time for peace.

You are not alone in your hope that peaceful existence can happen. Here are some suggestions for you to help bring about peace. Things you *can* do—at home, at school and in the community.

SIGN
UP
NOW

YOUNG
PEOPLE
FOR
PEACE

Teach

Peace

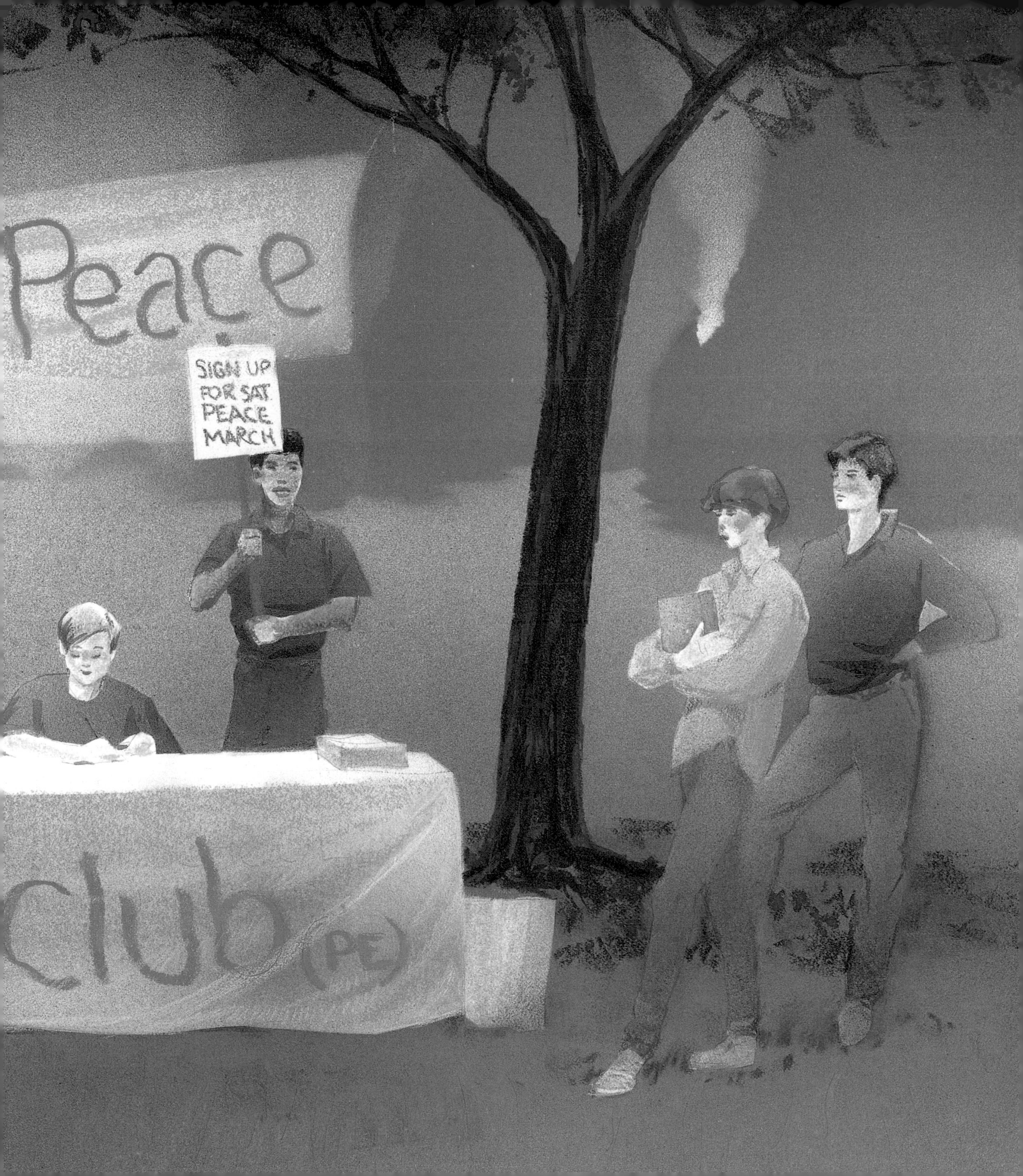
Peace
SIGN UP FOR SAT. PEACE MARCH
Club (PE)

Start a Peace Club

Get together with interested friends. Send a letter to them saying you want to start a peace club. Tell them you want to end war by organizing a group of people who will create activities that will promote peace. Suggest a few ideas that club members can get together and do:

- Write peace essays at school to be taken home to your parents.

- Correspond with peace pen pals from other countries.

- Start a peace camp in the summer and play peace games.

- Create your own International Children's Disarmament Day (see following page).

- Ask your teachers to teach peace education in your school.

- Write peace letters to world leaders.

A Sample Peace Letter

World leader's name
Address
City, State, Zip Code

Dear (President or World Leader) (Name):

We are a group of ___-year-olds. We look to you to lead us out of war. We look to you to create peace in the world. Can you help us? We are afraid of war. We don't want to grow up and kill people or be killed.

Do you have children of your own? Do you want them to become killers or be killed? Imagine your own child killing another human being or being killed by someone just as frightened? How would you feel?

We are a peace group in (town, state, country). We urge you to write back to us pledging your promise for world peace. We are going to collect letters and send them to the United Nations so everyone will be aware that you represent people who are peaceful and who want peace all over the world.

Will you write to us? We look forward to hearing from you.

With care,

The (name) Peace Group
(each person personally signs their name)
Your address
City, State and Zip Code

Children's Disarmament Day

Start a Children's Disarmament Day in your own city or town. My staff and I started the first American International Children's Disarmament Day in Middlebury, Vermont, U.S.A. A few years before, my wife and I took our students from the school we started (Education for Peace School) to Russia in what was then the Soviet Union. We wanted to meet with Russian students about peace. We traveled to Leningrad (now St. Petersburg) and Moscow and met with over 80 students from all over Russia. While I was there, I showed them my book for young people entitled *Tug of War: Peace Through Understanding Conflict.* One of the Russian adults, a former teacher, decided that she wanted to translate the book and find a publisher. She did, and now thousands of my books are published in that country.

One Russian man read what I was saying and let us know what he was doing to help Russian youth think and act in peaceful ways. He started the International Children's Disarmament Day and invited young people from all over Eastern Europe and the former Soviet Union to meet together and sign peace treaties that asked them not to buy war toys, not to ask their parents for such toys, and, when they grew up to be adults, to not use real weapons. It was a big success!

This Russian response inspired us to do the same thing here in the United States. We set up our own International  Disarmament Day in Vermont. We added our own special event —a War Toy Trade! Young people came together and traded in their war toys for intelligent, creative and peaceful toys. They also signed Peace Treaties and got a Peace Award for their participation. Over 500 people attended our first event!

You too can hold your own
International Children's Disarmament Day

For more information, write to us at: The Atrium Society, Education for Peace Project, P. O. Box 816, Middlebury, Vermont 05753 U.S.A. We will send you information on how to do one in your town! <u>OR</u> . . . If you're ready to turn your back on war, send us a *war toy* at the address above and we will send you the official *Atrium Peace Award*!

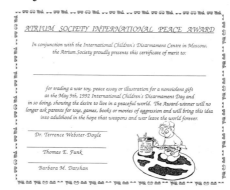

Here is something else you can do that will help people think of peace instead of becoming warriors. Have you ever noticed that in most cities and even small towns there is usually a war monument or memorial honoring a past war and the people killed in it? Sometimes it is a cannon from a former war, or an airplane or tank. Usually it has a large plaque with the names of those who died in the war and above that an iron statue of some war hero dressed in a military uniform, sometimes on a horse.

Why do we have these monuments to death? Why do we want to remember wars, killings, the destroying of homes and cities? Some people say that we must remember in order not to commit the same mistake in the future, that if each generation is shown the horrible atrocities of past wars, this will frighten them so that they will not go to war. But has this worked? Have these monuments to war stopped war? It seems that there is more and more violence despite the attempts of the people who built war monuments. And every country has them.

When I visited England and toured Eton School for boys, I was shocked to see rows and rows of long plaques covering the walls with hundreds and hundreds of young men's names who had died in World Wars I and II. It seemed so terribly sad that these young men were turned into warriors and died such violent and horrible deaths. The inscription that introduced these halls of dead men's names etched in iron plaques honored these graduates of the school as heroes, encouraging future generations to follow in their steps.

Perhaps we could erect peace monuments instead, honoring peace events and accomplishments. Doesn't this make

more sense? Do you know any heroes of peace we could honor?
Most "heroes" have been military or political leaders who have
fought or ordered people to fight in wars. Instead let's honor
real peace heroes.

I have one idea for a peace monument I would like to see.
It came out of our first International Children's Disarmament
Day. We collected many war toys traded in by young people for
nonviolent toys. Toward the end of the day, two boys approached to ask us if they could make a peace sculpture out of
the discarded toys. We thought it was a great idea. No one had
any idea what it would be until a few weeks later when the
boys and their father showed up at our office with a large peace
symbol (four feet by four feet) made of wood with the war toys
wired, nailed and glued to it. What a surprise! We take it with
us now to all our Education for Peace Day events to symbolize a
Monument for Peace.

What other monuments can you think of?

Chapter 17

WAKING UP FROM THE DREAM

Every day we are bombarded by a concept that we are so used to seeing it no longer affects us. It is a false concept and it is important for us to see the falseness in it every time it is presented to us.

This false concept is:
There are good guys and there are bad guys.

This image of bad guys and good guys is totally made up. It's only a dream. But we live this dream on a daily basis. It is fed to us by television—even in television commercials. It is drilled into us by movies—especially war stories, mysteries, horror movies and police stories. It is manufactured by the makers of war toys.

At school, on the job, at home—at one time or another
we look at someone we know and we think,
"That is a bad person. That bad person is my enemy."

This world of good guys and bad guys is *not real*. We have made it up, just like writers make up movie scripts. Have you noticed that there is no war or conflict when we go to sleep? That's because war is created by the way *we* think and act.

198

We've been conditioned to think that war is necessary. We have been trained to believe that we have enemies in the world and that the only way we can deal with them is by fighting with them, to become warriors and go to war with them.

If we look at these people we call "enemy"
without judging them, what do we see?
We see people, like us, who want love, attention,
the best for their families and friends.

Have you noticed that when you are enjoying a good day and you feel no fear, you have no enemies? The moment you feel fear about something—you feel conflict inside you. You want to run away. Or you want to fight! The moment you feel fear, there is someone or something you are afraid of, and that person or thing becomes your "enemy." You create this enemy in your mind, and this is the only place it exists. **This enemy is a dream—a figment of your imagination.**
Every time we look at someone and see an enemy, we instantly see differences between that person and ourselves. Every time we look at someone and see a friend, we immediately see similarities between us. When we see an enemy, we see "him/her vs. me." We see "them" vs. "us." When we see a friend, there is no "them"—only "us."

We will have peace when people of the world
can look upon one another and see no "them"—only us.

To wake up from this dream of "them vs. us," we need to become aware of how we *create* conflict and *prevent* peace.

A Spark of Enemy!

Remember: what triggers conflict is the creation of "Enemy." So, every time you feel that spark in your brain, "Enemy!"—all you have to do is ask yourself:

❶   Why have I created this image of Enemy?

❷   What am I afraid of?

❸   Is some physical harm about to come to me?

❹   Am I afraid of mental or psychological harm?

❺   Can I feel my survival instincts automatically working in me?

❻   Do I want to fight? Do I want to run away?

Then, when you've asked yourself those questions, take these steps:

❶   Understand that your desire to fight or run is good and natural! It's there to protect you from physical harm!

200

❷ Now stop! Put the spark out before it rages into a fire! Tell yourself, if you are not in *physical* danger, that *this creation of an enemy is no more than a thought in your brain—a* **mechanical** *reaction—a "dream" that is created by an electrochemical process in the brain.*

❸ Tell yourself that this thought in your brain is connected to the feeling of fear.

❹ Put on the brakes! Ask yourself: Can I stay awake, be alert and not be pulled into the "old" brain of primitive cave creatures? Can I actually see that the enemy, and therefore the need to defend myself by creating a warrior hero, is *only* a dream? A nightmare?

Learn to trust your observations and instincts. You know what to do!

**The only war there is
is in your head!
Wake up from the dream!**

WAR IS OVER FOREVER

Dear Reader,

Thank you for reading this book. As I said in the beginning, I wrote it so that you can live a more healthy, happy life by *understanding what influences create warriors and war*. The most important thing I can say is: Don't accept without question what another tells you to believe. We all need to question. Questioning creatively exercises that muscle between your ears. Without questioning, our brain becomes old very fast; like an unexercised muscle, it becomes soft and flabby. Remember that *we* have created our problems. They are not beyond us. We *can*, therefore, understand them! It takes work! But we can do it if we are truly serious and try hard. I hope you do, for your life and the life of all human beings.

If you want to write me about what you think of this book or your concerns about warriors and war, please feel free to do so at the following address. I would enjoy hearing from you:

Dr. Terrence Webster-Doyle
c/o The Atrium
PO Box 816
Middlebury, Vermont 05753 USA

With care,

Terrence Webster-Doyle

Dr. Terrence Webster-Doyle

Some Final Questions

1. Are the seeds of war within us?

2. Who is the enemy?

3. How do we create the enemy?

4. Can peace come about through war?

5. Do you believe that war is inevitable?

6. Who is responsible for war?

7. Can we fight violence with violence?

8. Do you think that solving conflict with violence is honorable?

9. Do you think playing with war toys can lead to using real war weapons as adults? Why?

10. How can somebody love *and* kill?

11. Are only men violent?

12. Who raises young boys to be warriors?

13. Does patriotism help bring about peace—or does it

only create more conflict?

14. Do you really know what it means to kill a person?

15. What would you kill for? Honor? Pride? Valor? Beliefs? A flag? To defend a country? Bravery? Glory? A job?

16. What does the saying, "Death before dishonor" mean?

17. What prevents peace?

18. What can you do to bring about peace?

19. Do you think it would help to have peace education classes at your school?

20. Should we outlaw war?

P.S. Let me leave you with the following story of peace.

Make Believe

Guns firing, people screaming, bombs falling—the enemy is on the run and *"we"* are the heroes. The screen shows the names of the actors and then goes blank as the lights come on and you slowly come back to being aware of yourself sitting in the theater with other young people.

Out in the street you still feel as if you were in the war,

that you were the hero—Sergeant Armstrong—the handsome, tough, cool, military man who fought to save his country, race and beliefs from the enemy. You feel a strange, powerful energy in your body as if you could now fight and conquer. You feel protective of your country, patriotic and loyal. You feel you belong, which makes you feel secure, safe.

As you walk down the city street teeming with people, you notice the difference between them. Different features, color of skin, size, ethnic backgrounds. You see some that remind you of the "enemy" you just saw in the movie. You feel yourself go tense at the sight of these "foreign" looking people. You feel distrust and fear. Remembering how Sergeant Armstrong mowed down the foreign enemies with his mighty M60 machine gun, you feel tall, strong and cool—a fighting man.

Stopping by the video arcade you go right to the Phantom Fighter's game and relive the "glory" of the battles of the famous wars. Your collection of military toys has been given up for real camouflage clothes you wear around on occasion. You dream of serving your country as a hero and a patriot. Your plan is to join the military after high school—perhaps even to make it a career. You have already read the recruiting materials promising glory and honor serving and defending *your* great nation. You feel a sudden feeling of pride as you consider this.

Taking the train out of the city, you travel home to the countryside. Walking from the station to your house, you take a short cut through some lovely woods. The tall trees reach up to the sun, as leaves reflect the light of the late afternoon. Some crickets are chirping; a squirrel scampers past you. The green grass underfoot softly cushions your walk. There are no sounds of traffic here, no movie theaters or video arcades, no military films or thoughts of glory. The wind suddenly moves the treetops above you; the rustling of leaves brushing against each other creates a magical calm.

Suddenly, you become aware of a delicate, sweet odor of honeysuckle. Looking to your left, you see a bush of lovely white flowers. Leaning over to smell one, you are enveloped by its enchanting scent. For a brief yet everlasting moment, "you" are gone! There is *only* that fragrance—nothing else. In the distance a train hoots its horn, the haunting sound echoing through the woods. For a brief yet everlasting moment all is well. There is peace. It has been there all the time.

Birds sing, crickets chirp, the wind moves through trees, and everything is right with the world.

The Dream is Over.

So Who *Is* The Enemy?

AFTERWORD:

A Message to Parents, Teachers, Counselors or Anyone Who Works or Lives with Young People

"Never doubt that a small group of thoughtful, committed citizens can change the world; indeed, it is the only thing that ever does."
— Margaret Mead

The intent of this book is to help young people understand the influences that mold them into warriors. Its fundamental question is, can we solve conflict without violence?

This book explores how warriors and war are created. It promotes the teaching of peace education in schools as a way to understand and resolve conflict at the primary level—that is to *prevent* it. I don't think I need recite all the horrific statistics about war or the cost of war in people and dollars. We have all heard this information many times before, and many of us are actively doing something about it.

There is no way to get around it: conflict is conflict. Individual conflict *is* global conflict. We create conflict by the way we think and act, by our primitive identification with the tribe, the country, the race, the belief system—all of which separate us as a human race, fragment us into opposing ideologies defending "ours" against "theirs."

We have created our own problems—and we can, therefore, understand and begin to do something about them. We have generally left understanding up to the "authorities," but the authorities cannot solve our problems for us or for our children. Understanding begins with us—the adults who live and work with children. It is our responsibility to help young people understand war and how one becomes a warrior. We spend so much time on reading, writing and arithmetic and practically none on a subject which ought to be the first and most important "R"—relationship.

The challenge for education in the twenty-first century is to help young people understand conflict in human relationship. This is a tremendously urgent demand—as anyone can see daily in the newspapers and on television. Books like this one speak directly to young people because, sadly, most adults don't seem to care—perhaps because many adults are so deeply attached to established beliefs in nation, race and religion they cannot find anything but controversy here. But those who really see the need to help our children will read these kinds of books and will take the time to sit down and work through them with young people.

To help young people get the most from this book, please help them do the activities that appear throughout the book—especially the sections on questioning. Learning by doing is very important, for two reasons:

1. Young people need to see that they can act in their homes, schools, community and in the world to bring about a more peaceful and humane way of life.

2. They also need to see that we adults do get actively involved in peace-related activities.

Some of what is written may seem difficult for them, but this is mainly because it is new. Please discuss parts they may not understand. It takes work, but they can understand it—although they may only understand it intellectually at first. Use personal examples from your own life to help them to see better that what they are reading and discussing is real.

What Else You Can Do

- Develop an understanding of the effects of war toys, movies and TV on children's behavior.

- Compile a resource list of persons, information and activities to promote peace (e.g., Educators for Social Responsibility in Cambridge, Massachusetts, USA).

- Give practical advice on how to be a conscientious objector.

- Write a letter to the editor of your local newspaper whenever you see war toys or activities that promote conflict.

- Write a letter to the editor of your local newspaper suggesting an Education for Peace Day in your community. Offer ideas and activities.

- Call or write your government leaders to protest war, war toys, and organizations that you feel promote war.

- Call or write your government leaders with ideas to promote peace—on the city streets, among neighbors, in communities, towns, cities and states.

- Contribute money, supplies or time to an Education for Peace organization.

Organizations That Can Help

Education for the People
(an independent student and youth newspaper)
NCUPI
1801 18th St. NW
Washington, DC 20009

Fund for Education and Training
(helps resisters of military draft registration)
800 18th Street NW, Suite 600
Washington, DC 20006

Psychologists for Social Responsibility
(a professional organization concerned with ending war)
1841 Columbia Road NW, Suite 209
Washington, DC 20009

Young and Teen Peacemakers
(a student run organization)
35 Lebanon Street
Hamilton, NY 13346

Youth against Militarism Project
Friends for a Nonviolent World
(student group concerned with student rights and social issues)
2025 Nicollet Avenue South #203
Minneapolis, MN 55404

Protest War Toys:

HASBRO Inc. (maker of G. I. Joe)
1027 Newport Avenue
Pawtucket, Rhode Island 02862

HASBRO Inc.
Regional Offices
32 West 23d Street
New York, New York 10010

Mattell Toys
5150 Rosecrans Avenue
Hawthorne, CA 90250

Nintendo of America, Inc.
PO Box 957
Redmond, Washington 98052

War Resisters League/New England
PO Box 1093
Norwich, CT 06360

War Resisters League
339 Lafayette Street
New York, New York 10012

The War Resisters League will send you lots of helpful information and ideas on starting your own Stop War Toys Campaign. They will also send information on where you can write to protest the production of war toys. Or you can write to us at:

The Atrium Society
Education for Peace Project
PO Box 816
Middlebury, Vermont 05753 USA

We will help you locate information on war toys, peace organizations, and conflict resolution activities, including organizing and giving an Children's Disarmament Day in your community.

Please remember that w*e can make a difference!* And by active involvement in peace education, we adults set the right example for our children. We show them it is possible to curtail warlike action. And more importantly, we show them it is possible to understand the primary causes of war and to prevent war from happening again—if we are serious and are willing to work at it each day. This is the greatest gift we can give them: a peaceful, happy, harmonious existence—not in theory, but in real life!

A CURRICULUM ON UNDERSTANDING WAR

War—What Is it Good For?
Educating for Peace

To end war and bring about peace, we need to create a new kind of education. Young men and women have been trained at school to make war. You and I can help create schools that make peace.

Atrium offers a comprehensive, interactive peace education curriculum for students aged twelve to fifteen—outlining daily classes, role-plays, questions and activities. It introduces young people to peaceful conflict resolution, self-understanding, personal relationship skills and today's global issues—and reflects Atrium's years of hands-on experience working with children, their parents and teachers. Twenty lessons, proven in public and independent school classrooms, counseling centers and other programs, explore these issues:

* ***Do I Fight or Do I Run?***
    Learning about the human brain and its fight-or-flight response to physical—and *psychological*—conflict.
* ***The Enemy: Someone Who Is Different***
    Understanding why people join and identify with particular groups—and how this creates personal and global conflict.
* ***Why Is Everybody Always Picking on Me?***
    Handling bullies peacefully, seeing the stress and hurt behind the bully and comparing interpersonal and international bullying.
* ***Operation Warhawks: War and Peace Issues for Young People***;
    Revealing biological and social conditioning behind the creation of warriors, looking at military recruiting, training and combat service and presenting young people with peaceful alternatives.

If you are interested in this Peace Education curriculum, please contact us at the Atrium.

215

Peace comes about
through education;
war comes about through
ignorance.

Is there a choice?

PEACE EDUCATION WORKSHOPS
AND COMPANION RESOURCES

Thank you for reading OPERATION WARHAWKS. If you are interested in the companion series to this book—the four-part Education for Peace series—the books are listed below. All the books show how to resolve conflict nonviolently and present constructive ways young people can peacefully confront hostile aggression. They go deeply into the causes of individual and global conflict. Together the books complement the curriculum—*War: What Is It Good For?* Atrium publishes a journal for adults interested in peace education and nonviolent conflict resolution. If you are interested in the curriculum, journals or teacher-training seminars, please contact us.

Education for Peace workshops developed by Dr. Terrence Webster-Doyle present a unique, integrated approach to conflict resolution, using the combined principles of education, psychology and the seemingly contradictory study of the Martial Arts. The intent is to educate the public about the fundamental causes of conflict, individually and globally. In the interest of a peaceful classroom, home and world, we must learn to recognize the destructive, conditioned attitudes and beliefs in society that perpetuate conflict and—at the same time—understand the basic causes of confusion and conflict within the individual. Tailored to the individual needs of the sponsors, the workshop will:

1. Help the sponsor educate and serve its community by creating a more humane and intelligent understanding of conflict.

2. Demonstrate peaceful conflict resolution—individual and global.

3. Enhance the sponsor's existing and future programs by bringing its community innovative ideas and activities in understanding conflict.

4. Train its educators and parents of young students to implement

these ideas and activities in their daily lives, at school and at home, in exciting and effective ways.

5. Give the sponsor an opportunity to raise funds through seminar tuition and book sales.

Based on the Internationally Acclaimed, Award-Winning Education for Peace Book Series:

- TUG OF WAR: *Peace through Understanding Conflict*

- FIGHTING THE INVISIBLE ENEMY: *Understanding the Effects of Conditioning*

- WHY IS EVERYBODY ALWAYS PICKING ON ME? *A Guide to Handling Bullies*

- FACING THE DOUBLE-EDGED SWORD: *The Art of Karate for Young People*

Award-Winning Books
by Dr. Terrence Webster-Doyle

For young people:

Operation Warhawks: *How Young People Become Warriors*

THE EDUCATION FOR PEACE SERIES (ages 7-15)

Tug of War: *Peace Through Understanding Conflict*
Fighting the Invisible Enemy: *Understanding the Effects of Conditioning*
Facing the Double-Edged Sword: *The Art of Karate for Young People*
Why Is Everybody Picking on Me: *A Guide to Handling Bullies*

THE MARTIAL ARTS FOR PEACE SERIES (ages 10-17)

Eye of the Hurricane: *Tales of the Empty-Handed Masters*
Maze of the Fire Dragon: *Tales of the Empty-Handed Masters*
Flight of the Golden Eagle: *Tales of the Empty-Handed Masters*

For adults:

Karate: *The Art of Empty Self*
One Encounter, One Chance: *The Essence of the Art of Karate*

THE SANE AND INTELLIGENT LIVING SERIES

Growing up Sane: *Understanding the Conditioned Mind*
Brave New Child: *Education for the 21st Century*
The Religious Impulse: *A Quest for Innocence*
Peace—The Enemy of Freedom: *The Myth of Nonviolence*

ABOUT THE AUTHOR

Dr. Terrence Webster-Doyle was Founder and Director of three independent schools and has taught at the secondary, community college and university levels in Education, Psychology and Philosophy. He has worked in juvenile delinquency prevention and has developed counseling programs for teenagers. He has earned a doctorate degree in Psychology, has produced numerous conferences on "New Directions in Education," and was Director of the Center for Educational Alternatives in Northern California. Dr. Webster-Doyle gives workshops internationally for both young people and adults on the issues of conditioning, conflict, and its peaceful resolution. In 1992 Austria's Albert Schweitzer Society awarded Dr. Webster-Doyle the Robert Burns Medal in Literature for "outstanding merit in the field of peace-promotion." He is the author of fourteen books.

Dr. Terrence Webster-Doyle and Rod Cameron can be contacted through the Atrium Society. (See address and phone number on facing page.)

ABOUT THE ARTIST

Rod Cameron was born in 1948 in Chicago, Illinois, but has lived in southern California most of his life. He studied painting with the renowned illustrator, Keith Ward, and at the Otis/Parsons School of Design in Los Angeles, California.

Mr. Cameron has been designing and illustrating for over twenty years; his work has been shown on major network television and has received seventeen awards for illustrative excellence.

ABOUT THE PUBLISHER

Atrium Society concerns itself with fundamental issues which prevent understanding and cooperation in human affairs. Starting with the fact that we are conditioned by our origin at birth, our education and our experiences, the intent of the Atrium Society is to bring this issue of conditioning into the forefront of our awareness. Observation of the fact of conditioning—becoming directly aware of the movement of thought and action—brings us face-to-face with the actuality of ourselves. Seeing who we actually are, not merely what we think we are, reveals the potential for a transformation of our ways of being and relating.

If you would like more information, please write or call us. We enjoy hearing from people who read our books, and we appreciate your comments.

Atrium Society
P.O. Box 816
Middlebury, Vermont 05753
Tel: (802) 388-0922
Fax: (802) 388-1027
For book order information:
(800) 848-6021

SPECIAL BOOK DISCOUNTS

Atrium extends special low prices to public and independent schools, libraries, youth centers and other educational customers who buy our peace education books in bulk quantities. Discounts apply both to the "Education for Peace" books for young people and to adult titles suitable for teacher training, parenting and adult education.

MARTIAL ARTS FOR PEACE

In addition to his experience and credentials in education, Dr. Terrence Webster-Doyle brings a unique perspective to his conflict-resolution and peace-education work with young people: he has studied and taught Karate for over 30 years and holds a sixth-degree Black Belt. Founder and Chief Instructor of Take Nami Do Karate, he is dedicated to promoting the art of Karate as a means for self-understanding and of confident, nonviolent avoidance of physical conflict. Seemingly contradictory to the aims of peaceful conflict resolution, a martial art—if properly taught—reveals itself as a safe, fun, healthy and direct way for young people to see conflict within themselves, gain self-esteem, and use their new insights and confidence to *avoid fighting*.

Atrium Society works to bring together people who, and resources that, give an intelligent perspective to the Martial Arts as a tool for the understanding of conflict. Its comprehensive "Martial Arts for Peace" program helps create an understanding of the martial arts as a way to peace, assisting young students in their education about relationship—what it means to live with dignity, caring and beauty in their daily lives. The Atrium Society disseminates thought-provoking and insightful information about the creative aspects of martial arts, through literature, videotapes, classes, workshops and conferences.

Classes for young people, teens and adults are offered in Vermont and in northern California. The "Martial Arts for Peace" project also encourages martial arts schools, youth centers, and schools nationwide to host Dr. Webster-Doyle's workshops for young people. For information on these activities or for special instructor-training programs and the forthcoming Vermont "Martial Arts for Peace" summer camp, please contact:

Atrium Society/"Martial Arts for Peace"
PO Box 816
Middlebury VT 05753 USA
Tel: (802) 388-0922;   Fax (802) 388-1027

International Praise for Dr. Terrence Webster-Doyle's Previous Books for Young People— the "Education for Peace" Series:

The award-winning "Education for Peace" books have earned widespread acclaim as resources for the understanding and nonviolent resolution of conflict.

- Dr. Webster-Doyle has been awarded the Robert Burns Medal for Literature by Austria's Albert Schweitzer Society, for "outstanding merits in the field of peace-promotion."

- Chosen as a focus of, and highly praised at, the International Congress of Teachers for Peace, in Paris, France.

- The books have been placed on permanent display at the Museum of World Peace and Solidarity, in Samarkand, Uzbekhistan.

- Winner of Benjamin Franklin Awards for Excellence in Independent Publishing

- "These topics are excellent and highly relevant. If each of the major countries of the world were to have ten Drs. Webster-Doyle, world peace is guaranteed to be achieved over a period of just one generation." —Dr. Charles Mercieca, Executive Vice-President International Assoc'n of Educators for World Peace NGO, United Nations, UNICEF & UNESCO

- Acclaimed at the Soviet Peace Fund Conference in Moscow; published in Russia by Moscow's Library of Foreign Literature and Magistr Publications

- *Why is Everybody Always Picking on Me?* —cited by the *Omega New Age Directory* as one of the Ten Best Books of 1991

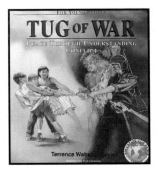 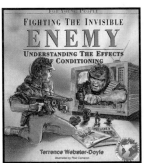